WORKING
A · N · D
MANAGING

IN · A
NEW AGE

WORKING
A·N·D
MANAGING

IN·A
NEW AGE

Ron Garland

HUMANICS NEW AGE
P. O. Box 7447
Atlanta, Georgia 30309

TM

Humanics New Age
P. O. Box 7447
Atlanta, Georgia 30309

Copyright© 1989 by Humanics Limited.
Humanics New Age is an imprint of Humanics Limited.
No part of this book may be reproduced by any means,
nor transmitted, nor translated into a machine language,
without written permission from Humanics Limited.

7/90

First Printing

PRINTED IN THE UNITED STATES OF AMERICA

Library of Congress Cataloging - in- Publication Data

Garland, Ron, 1948-
  Working and Managing in a New Age.
  Bibliography: p.
  1. Organizational effectiveness. 2. Job enrichment.
3. Job satisfaction. 4. Work environment. I. Title.
HD58. 9. G37 1988   658. 3'14   88-31966
ISBN 0-89334-123-1

Cover design by PURNA AHUJA

Edited by ROBERT GRAYSON HALL

To Ashleigh Brilliant

Table of Contents

Unconditional, Unlimited Lifetime Guarantee

This book comes with an unprecedented, absolute, total, 100%, lifetime guarantee as noted below:

POT-SHOTS NO. 1198.

MY TEACHINGS
ARE GUARANTEED
TO BE
SATISFACTORY,

Ashleigh
Brilliant

OR
YOU MAY HAVE
ALL YOUR OLD
BELIEFS BACK.

Acknowledgements

To Don, Coletta, Dale, Grace, Herman, Elizabeth, Virginia, Kelly, Geneva, Roy, Craig, Rick, Gary, Terry, Pam, Carl, Trula, Bill, and Judy for many interesting lessons in human relations.

To Alan Watts, Marilyn Ferguson, and Rick Fields for insightful books which have helped to create a meaningful context.

To Gary for unleashing me on the world of personnel management and Alda for teaching me so much about employee relations.

To the thousands of good managers, hard-working employees, and dedicated union officials I have encountered over the past two decades, who have provided so much valuable first-hand experience, and to the thousands of bad managers, indifferent employees, and obstructionist union officials who have clearly demonstrated what doesn't work and why.

Finally, to Rhonda whose unreasonable behavior during "the terrible twos" gave me so much insight into dealing with fanatics in both the union and management.

CHAPTER ONE

The Dawn of the New Age

We live in the final, irretrievable crisis of industrialism. And as the industrial age passes into history, a new age is born.
— Alvin Toffler, *The Third Wave*

We are now entering a period of transition as significant as the transition from an agricultural to an industrial society. Whether it is labeled the "information society" or given any other name, it will require a new set of management priorities and practices.
— Lawrence M. Miller, *American Spirit: Visions of a New Corporate Culture*

The Age of Transition

We are at a turning point. We are experiencing a period of change unprecedented in human history. At first, the changes seemed overwhelming and incomprehensible. During the 1960's and 1970's, many of us felt that a new era was dawning, but we didn't fully understand what was happening or why. It was only in the 1980's that we began to sense the direction and magnitude of the change.

There have now been several excellent, comprehensive analyses of this historical "turning point." One by Fritjof Capra was even titled *The Turning Point*. Marilyn Ferguson described the implications and scope of this period of transformation better than anyone in her outstanding book *The Aquarian Conspiracy*. Alvin Toffler brilliantly examined many aspects of this emerging new world in his books *Future Shock* and *The Third Wave*. John Nesbitt focused upon the general patterns of change in *Megatrends*, and then specifically looked at how all these changes are impacting corporations in his insightful book *Re-inventing the Corporation*. Many others have also attempted to put our age into context and make some sense of it all.

Whether we term the modern age as The Third Wave, The Turning Point, The Age of Aquarius, The Post-Industrial Society, The Age of Information, The Space Age, The Age of Change, or The Age of Transition, there is now a general understanding of the meaning and importance of this era. We can now see that, historically speaking, we are in the very first few seconds of the first minute of the first day of the dawn of a New Age. The day has not yet arrived in all its glory. Noon is still decades away. We are still under the influence of the preceding night to a significant degree, but the New Day has arrived and its impact (sunshine) will continue to spread.

Some may believe the term "New Age" simply refers to the movement towards integrating ancient concepts from Eastern religious-philosophies (such as Tao, Zen and Buddhism) with modern Western science. While this trend is an important part of the New Age, the New Age is much more. It includes "New Thought" Christian schools, the Human Potential Movement, and impacts virtually every major religion. Even the Catholic Church has produced a noted "New Age" prophet in Pierre Teilhard de Chardin.

There are many aspects to the New Age—political, social, economic, religious, etc. The New Age is reflected in part in virtually every major social movement of our times including the women's movement, the civil rights movement, the new quest for direct spirituality, the peace movement, environmentalism, the sexual revolution, the computer revolution, the struggle for social and economic justice, etc. The New Age involves a whole new pattern of thinking about human existence itself. This new thought pattern is frequently referred to as the New Age Paradigm.

We are, in fact, experiencing a radical paradigm shift. We are developing a new conceptual framework for viewing the world and our place in it. This new mindset is at the very heart of the New Age. We are shifting away from Cartesian science, Newtonian physics, and the mechanistic view of life and towards a new physics based upon Einstein's theories and a system's view of life based upon concepts of unity and wholeness. The information explosion has forced us to integrate new knowledge with our old points of views. There is more information available today than at any time in recorded history. This not only includes "new" information from scientific research and computer assisted analysis, but for the first time "ancient" knowledge from all around the world is available simultaneously at one place and one time for our consideration. All this information from modern and ancient sources has allowed us to see the world from a much broader and deeper perspective than was possible for the people in the past.

In America, the initial paradigm or conceptual framework for most of us was the post-war, industrial based perspective of the 1950's. This was our basic thesis. The information explosion and value shifts of the 1960's and 1970's produced an antithesis (and to some extent an overreaction which lead down many erroneous paths). Now, in the 1980's and 1990's, we are merging the old and the new and producing a new synthesis which will become the conceptual framework for the people of the 21st Century.

The focus of this book will be upon the changes occurring in work and management as part of the broader New Age Transformation. Many different concepts have been advanced to explain the how, what, and why of the new paradigm. The New Age is frequently referred to as the "Post-Industrial Era," or "The Age of Information." This is a useful starting point. One need not be a Marxist to understand the impact the economic system has on all aspects of society.

In the Western World, (and especially in the United States), the economic structure has changed radically over the past four decades. We have moved from an Industrial Age to an Information Age. The office has replaced the factory as the primary work site. Today's work force is much more likely to work with information and ideas than bolts and wrenches. In order to work and manage effectively in the Information Age, we must abandon the outmoded management style of the factory environment and devise realistic approaches that fit the new information work force. Companies and organizations that don't adapt to the demands of the New Age will cease to exist. This book will discuss the necessary changes that organizations must make in order to be effective in the post-industrial world.

What is so "New" about New Age Management?

Many of the concepts discussed herein are not all that new. They have been around for decades. You have heard of many of the ideas before and heard them lumped together in various packages, such as "Theory Y management" or "humanistic management," or more recently "Theory Z management," "vanguard management" or "Third Wave management." Even during the heyday of the American Industrial Era (the late 1940's, 1950's, and early 1960's), it was clear to many thoughtful observers that the traditional management approach was not the best way to run a human organization.

However, during this post-World War II period, the United States held a virtual monopoly in many areas of production. The War had destroyed the industrial base of most of Europe and Japan. If someone wanted a bus, car, plane, radio, or television, they bought it from the United States. Having no real competition, American businesses succeeded even with poor management practices.

Then, the world began to change. Europe became more competitive. Japan, Korea, Hong Kong, and Taiwan started becoming competitive in international markets. Soon the American Industrial Society was in full decline. After a long, hard period of re-examination and comparison with our competition, (especially the Japanese), we have learned many painful lessons.

The three major lessons are as follows. One, we have ceased to be an industrial society and have become an information society. We are unlikely to ever return to world dominance in industrial production. Two, to be successful and effective in our remaining industries and in our new information agencies, services, and high-tech enterprises, we must work and manage differently. A lot differently.

Three, the post-World War II period has also seen a dramatic shift of functions from the private sector (family and churches) to the public

4

sector (including local, state, and federal government). For our society to work, the public sector must also function effectively. Therefore, the public sector also needs to adapt to the New Age Management requirements and adopt the new approaches that are being slowly and somewhat reluctantly accepted in the corporate and business communities.

The Baby Boomers: The Continuing Explosion

It is not entirely coincidental that the New Age arrived with the Baby Boom generation. There had always been those who questioned the traditional worldview and traditional way of doing things. However, with the Baby Boomers we now have a substantial segment of society refusing to accept tradition for tradition's sake. The Baby Boomers are always looking for something new and something better. They have a belief in progress, a commitment to change, and a willingness to experiment unparalleled in human history. By virtue of their sheer numbers, they have had an explosive impact on each stage of life that they pass through from childhood through adolescence, early adulthood and now, as they near the stage where they will assume formal leadership of virtually all of society. The large numbers of Baby Boomers have made them a "critical mass." (A "critical mass" is when enough people think the same way to have a dramatic impact on society. One person changing a point of view may not produce any impact. A thousand may not produce any notable impact. But a million people changing their "mindset" or thought pattern may become a critical mass which fundamentally alters society, even though they are not an outright majority.)

There are two basic reasons for the current ascendency of New Age Management. First of all, it works. It is a more effective way to run an organization. Secondly, the Baby Boomers are demanding it. It fits their new values and their lifestyles. These two factors go hand-in-hand. If New Age Management didn't work, it wouldn't matter so much that the Baby Boomers like it. However, the fact that it works would not be enough if there wasn't a new generation of workers/leaders predisposed towards using it.

Most managers from the pre-war (World War II) generations are not in tune with this new management philosophy. Most of them would rather struggle along with the poor to mediocre results produced by the traditional management techniques than adapt to a more effective system that would require them to change their attitudes. They will continue to resist New Age Management for another decade or two until they are dead or living in Sun City retirement homes. But the "Old Age" approaches will pass away as these people pass into their own old ages. Already their influence is declining significantly as the New Age management philosophy is being utilized more and more each day.

The way this First New Age Generation relates to authority is especially important to work and management. Just as the Boomers challenged their parents (the generation gap), their schools (the student revolts), and the political and religious authorities (Make Love, Not War), the Baby Boomers also challenge the traditional authority of the employer. If you order a Baby Boomer to jump, you'll more likely hear "why?," than the traditional "how high?"

Dr. Moris Massey, a professor and lecturer from Colorado, has an excellent series of video presentations which briefly and clearly discuss this trend called "What You Are Is Where You Were When." Massey explains that a radical shift in values occurred in the post-World War II period and that the Baby Boomers' view of work (and the world) is so fundamentally different from preceding generations that it is impossible to successfully manage them in the traditional ways. He notes that as a result of their unique "value programming", Boomers expect work to be fun and meaningful—two ideas that seldom occurred to older generations when considering work.

It is extremely difficult for the older generation to accept the idea (much less act upon it) that work should be fun and meaningful. To the older generation, you worked to make money. The Boomers also want money, but they want much more; they want to have fun and find meaning while making it. They already are the dominant generation in lower and middle management and most technical positions. To get maximum effectiveness from the Boomers, the work environment must provide fun and meaning. Managers who fail to understand and act upon this new reality will never be able to manage effectively. They will not be good leaders, but office cops fighting a losing battle.

The older generation of government and business leaders have tried to blame declining American productivity on the Baby Boomers, alleging that the Boomers don't have the "work ethic." This is partly true, but partly misleading.

The Boomers don't have the *traditional* work ethic. The traditional work ethic was based largely upon fear—fear of being fired, fear of being laid off, fear of a depression, fear of starving, fear of economic collapse, etc. Boomers were raised during unprecedented prosperity. They are not easily motivated by the old fears (even very valid fears) of previous generations.

The problem with productivity occurred when the Boomers entered the work force and were managed by traditional managers using traditional (fear based) assumptions and techniques. The gap between a management style based upon fear, negative assumptions, and traditional values and the Boomers' work patterns based upon positive expectations and changing values created a crisis in the work place and combined with many other factors to lower productivity.

Now that the Boomers are beginning to emerge en masse into the middle and top management levels, the old management styles will be scrapped. The traditionalists who couldn't understand the Boomers as employees are going to be absolutely stunned to see the changes that the Boomers make once they attain full power. The New Age will not truly begin to bloom until the Baby Boomers take power from the Presidency of the United States to the CEO's of all the major corporations.

The Boomer's impact has been felt by many of those close to them in age. Thus, many people born during the war years, 1940 to 1945, have come to accept the values of this generation and think of themselves as Boomers also. In fact, the appeal of being a Boomer is so great for some politicians that a few of them born in the late 1930's are even claiming to be Baby Boomers and offering themselves as candidates for the New Age. The first of the literal Baby Boomers will be 44 in 1990. Within the next 10 to 20 years, the Boomers will enter their 50's and 60's (the age group that normally wields the most power in a society). At this point, the Boomers will achieve their maximum impact. And, for better or worse, the world will never be the same again. Or, in the words of a leading exponent of the traditionalist camp, Ronald Reagan, "You ain't seen nothing yet."

New Agers and Old Agers

Many writers refer to those people who see the world through the new paradigm as "New Agers," and those people who still use the old paradigm as "Old Agers." This is not a reference to a person's age, but to the conceptual framework which he/she uses to understand the world. A New Ager may be 70 and an Old Ager may be 22. These terms are simply another attempt to briefly refer to the people with these two different mindsets. (Other commonly used terms for New Agers are "transcenders" and "transformers." I may occasionally use one of these words, but I don't like them. I especially dislike "Old Ager" as it carries a very negative connotation.)

One of the basic points of New Age Management is that you should not personalize criticism, i.e. you criticize the idea or the behavior, but not the person. There is certainly a lot to criticize in the Old Ager's ideas and behavior. But they are still human beings and deserve respect and decent treatment. Many of them are very nice, well-meaning people. Many of them are friends and relatives. And many of them are very frightened by New Age ideas. Consistently referring to them in derogatory terms is not conducive to enhancing communications and helping them understand the New Age Paradigm to the extent that they are able. Therefore, I will generally use the term "traditionalist" in referring to the those who use the old paradigm of the industrial age, since this term is one that many of them use themselves.

Maximum Minimization or Minimum Maximization

You will see words like "maximize" and "minimize" frequently in this book. This is in recognition of the fact that it is generally impossible to increase any positive aspect to 100% or lower any negative aspect to 0%. For example, there will always be employees who are just plain "turkeys." No approach will succeed with them, and there will be no choice but to terminate them. There will always be some unpleasant tasks that cannot be turned into fun. There will always be a few meaningless reports. There will always be a degree of unfairness—attractive people will always have an edge over unattractive people, etc. Therefore, rather than trying to do the impossible and achieve 100% of the positive features and have 0% negative features, we focus upon realistic expectations and advocate merely trying to maximize the positive and minimize the negative. You should not become depressed because you are unable to eliminate all negative aspects from the work environment and create a totally positive situation 100% of the time. No one has ever done it. If an employer did succeed in creating a work environment that was perfect without any negative features whatsoever, then employees would be paying employers to be able to work (play) there. One of the reasons they call it "work" is that the worker is doing at least some things he/she would not normally do just for fun. For example, a person who loves ice cream (don't we all) may take a job as an ice cream taster for an ice cream company. This person may have enjoyed eating two or three ice cream treats a day in the past just for fun. However, eating ice cream eight hours a day, five days a week will soon become "work." This is not something a person would do every day just for fun. The person may still consider this a good job, but there will be times during the day when tasting another ice cream will be the last thing that person wants to do. And yet he/she must do it to do the job properly.

So strive for the possible, maximize the positive, minimize the negative, and recognize that all jobs will have some undesirable features.

Overview Not Overkill

This small book is intended as an introduction to the major New Age concepts related to work and management. This is not a comprehensive analysis. I hope to show that a progressive approach to work/management is important, interesting, and fun. Many other sources of information and recommended readings which you should read and explore will be listed in the "Recommended Reading" section at the end of the book.

This book is also meant to be used and re-used as a quick reference to key concepts. It is not padded with irrelevant verbiage. It is a concise statement of the key principles of working and managing in the New Age which should help workers and managers maintain proper focus. Without a context, work, (and life), has no meaning. This is an effort to create such a context so you can understand the meaning of work in your life.

Caution: This Book is Not Value Neutral

This book is not an objective analysis. It doesn't pretend to be a scholarly study. It is partly a report of what is happening, but even more so, it is an argument for what should be happening and what must happen if organizations are to be effective in the future. The book is not value free. I admit openly to being an advocate of progressive, humanistic, effective, enjoyable, New Age approaches to work and management.

How Shall We Manage to Work This?

This book deals with work from the viewpoint of both worker and manager. It will address ways managers can create a more positive environment for their workers and ways workers can create a more positive environment for themselves—even in places where their managers are traditionalists. We will begin by discussing the work environment from the standpoint of managers. It might have made more sense to begin with work from the worker's perspective, since every employee is a worker, but not all employees are managers. Managers are also employees who report to other managers and have the same problems and concerns dealing with their own managers that workers have with first-line supervisors.

However, despite the fact that all employees are workers, we will begin with a discussion of work from the managers' point of view because it is primarily management that creates the work environment of any organization. Therefore, we will first consider the type of environment managers should be creating. Then, we will consider ways in which workers can seek to impact the work environment, modify attitudes, and achieve their objectives within both positive and negative work environments.

Now, Let's Get to Work and Have Some Fun

The New Age Manager believes in fun. Therefore, a book on New Age Management should also be fun. We will intersperse the text with periodic cartoons. The cartoons support our central concept of combining fun and effectiveness as they also serve both purposes—adding some fun while helping to emphasize a serious point.

CHAPTER TWO

Better Living Through Better Management: Creating the New, Improved Work Environment

> *What we need, therefore, is to revise the concept and practice of work in such a way that it becomes meaningful and fulfilling for the individual worker, useful for society, and part of the harmonious order of the eco-system. To reorganize and practice our work in this way will allow us to recapture its spiritual essence.*
> —Fritjof Capra, *The Turning Point*

POT-SHOTS NO. 811.

Don't let them
poison your mind
with ideas about

Love
and
Brotherhood.

Ashleigh Brilliant

What is Your Management Philosophy?

Ask the above question to most managers and they will likely stare at you as if you were slightly bananas. While all managers have a philosophy, many probably don't know it and can't explain it to you. They have generally just accepted whatever management philosophy existed in their organization when they arrived and have tried to work with it over the years for better or worse. While they undoubtedly understand that there are many different ways of doing things, they probably have never tried to put their approach to work or management into a comprehensive philosophy or context.

In the past, a fragmented, unexamined management philosophy may have been tolerable, but not today. Today, it is imperative that managers have a coherent, comprehensive, well-thought-out management philosophy and apply it consistently. Otherwise, they will lose out to those managers who do understand what they are doing and why.

If the question above were changed to "What is your management style?," then we would be more likely to get an answer. A manager might answer, "I'm a tough manager. I don't take no bull." Or someone might respond, "I'm an easy going person. I leave people alone and let them do their jobs. I only intervene when I absolutely must. I like to be friends with my people." At least this question gets managers thinking about their approach to management, but only in a very limited way. It is important for the effective manager to go beyond personal style and understand basic concepts related to work and management.

The manager is responsible for creating the work environment. The work environment is a small social system. In effect, the manager is creating a social system. A good manager will create a positive social system consistent with his/her role and values for the society at large. A democratic society which supports equality, fraternity, liberty, and justice for all, needs managers to support these same concepts within the work system.

Good Managers As Social Revolutionaries

Many honorable, intelligent, decent advocates for a just society see the philosophy and techniques of management as a rather boring topic with no relevance to their quest. They would sooner take a class on traditional Japanese basket weaving than a class on management. They see management classes as something of relevance only to the MBA types who are learning the latest management approaches in order to make big bucks for themselves while manipulating more workers. Most of these cynics are themselves workers and many even manage some kind of organization, but they would never waste time reading a book on management. This attitude on the part of many good people is most unfortunate. It leaves management in the hands of those people whose primary (almost exclusive) concern is financial and who put narrow economic interests above human considerations.

One of my major themes is the importance of good managers for a good society. Work is a major aspect of most people's lives. It not only determines their economic standard of living but plays a significant part in their levels of personal satisfaction, self-respect, self-esteem, self-development, etc. In addition, there is a high correlation between efficiency and prosperity in a society and that society's level of personal, social, political, and religious freedom. People committed to social progress need to understand that good management is a vital element in achieving those personal and social objectives. A poorly managed work system will have negative impacts at both the personal level (on the lives of individual workers) and the social level (by undermining the efficiency of the economy and threatening freedom and justice for all). On the other hand, a well managed work system will have positive benefits at both the individual level and social level.

Bad management results in poor employee morale, poor quality, low productivity, and unnecessary employee-employer conflicts, all of which produce economic decline which makes social progress and personal development difficult, if not impossible. Good management can create high morale, high quality, high productivity, a sense of purpose and meaning, minimize conflicts and maximize cooperation, create a sense of community, and foster self-respect, all of which lead to an improving economy which lays an excellent foundation for personal development and social progress.

One way of understanding this point is to apply Maslow's hierarchy of needs for individuals to the larger society. Within this analysis, just as individuals must first meet physical needs, security needs, and survival needs before being able to move on to the self-development and self-actualization needs, the society must first meet its economic needs before it can make significant progress in the areas of political freedom, individual dignity, and social justice. (This is, of course, very oversimplified and represents one of the many problems of Marxism. Maslow himself later recognized his hierarchy of needs theory was an oversimplification at the individual level and that all individuals are not locked into any one sequential pattern. Some individuals can and do pursue multiple levels simultaneously rather than sequentially or even use a different sequence. The same is also true of societies.)

The important point is that we need; A. (economic security), B. (individual freedom), and C. (social justice). The typical pattern and apparently the easier pattern has been A., then B., then C. Other sequential patterns may be possible, but without all three the society will be unstable and may end up with none of the three. How many societies can you think of which have a high degree of individual freedom and social justice and do not have an efficient economic system? Whether economic progress is the first, second, or third priority, it is an essential element in a free, just society.

Therefore, studying effective management techniques is not wasting time on irrelevant matters or abandoning the progressive movement, but rather learning the tools to promote the movement for a better future. (Good management is almost as important to a society as good parenting, and that is saying something, since we all know that the old cliche is true—the hand that rocks the cradle rules the world.) A more progressive management philosophy is vital to the New Age. A good manager should not be considered of lesser importance than artists, writers, political activists, environmental advocates, social reformers, etc. Management of private and public organizations is too important to be left to the traditionalists. Good management is a vehicle for social change and social progress. Good managers are really social revolutionaries.

The Three Foundations of Traditional Management Philosophy

In his book *Theory Z*, William Ouchi makes a very interesting point—a point which is rather obvious upon reflection, but one which is somewhat startling to those of us whose concept of early history begins with Howdy Doody. The point Ouchi makes is that until approximately 1840 and the beginning of the national railroads, there were no middle managers, at least not in business. Large corporations are a recent historical development. Prior to the industrial revolution, businesses were generally managed directly by the owner. The owner generally worked in, as well as supervised, the business. There were no layers of managers between owner and employee. Remember Tiny Tim's father worked directly for Ebenezer Scrooge. Scrooge didn't rely upon middle managers to do his dirty deeds for him. He abused his employees personally.

Prior to the industrial revolution and the corporation, there were very few large-scale, or even medium sized, organizations. In point of fact, throughout most of history there were only three types of large organizations, and they laid the traditional framework for managing and running organziations. These three were the churches, governments, and armies.

The Demilitarized Zone

The traditional management approach is primarily based upon the military model. Historically, armies were among the first wide-spread, large-scale organizations. The military model of a hierarchal commander with the soldier (worker) as an expendable resource has a long tradition. There was and still is very little participatory democracy in the military hierarchy. (This is not necessarily a criticism of the military model. This approach makes sense within the context of combat where command decisions must be made instantly in life and death situations. The problem is applying the military model to the modern office environment.) Today, as we move towards a new management philosophy, we are in effect demilitarizing our organizations.

The Divine Rights of Kings

Government bureaucracies existed in large measure to collect taxes for the King. In these bureaucracies, all power was vested in the King who, according to the King's self serving theory, derived his authority directly from God. The King, having absolute power, was not generally too interested in sharing the decision making process with his peasant subjects. Today, this idea of absolute power is recognized as absurd. Neither the President of the United States nor the leader of the Soviet Union can issue a directive and be certain that the bureaucracy will carry it out. All leaders in all types of government must utilize new techniques to insure that the government functions in the desired manner. Issuing edicts isn't enough.

Papal Infallibility

There was a time when the Catholic Church was the most powerful organization in the world. For centuries, it was the only large-scale, multi-national organization on the planet. A primary concept within the Church was that of Papal Infallibility. The Pope, no matter who he was, was always right, even if his position contradicted the last Pope. The Pope possessed all wisdom, all knowledge, all truth. His positions were not subject to debate or discussion. To disagree with the Pope was to risk a visit from the friendly neighborhood inquisitor. Given the centuries of Papal authority and power, this model of the church played a large role in establishing the foundations of the management philosophy for running secular organizations.

Today, the Pope has great difficulty keeping Catholics in line, and his so-called infallibility is considered an outright joke among most non-Catholics. Yet, this legacy of the all knowing leader at the top of the organization continues to influence traditional management practices. In the New Age, workers and managers alike understand that there is frequently more knowledge and wisdom about an organization at the bottom than at the top.

All three foundations of traditional management involve a subject-object approach or an "us versus them" attitude. The roles of leaders and followers are clearly defined, and leaders and followers are clearly separate. There is a distinct hierarchy.

Having looked briefly at the foundations of the traditional management philosophy, now let us look quickly at the foundations of New Age Management.

Zen and the Art of Management

The major foundation of New Age Management is the concept of *unity*. Unity is a central concept in two of the pillars of the New Age paradigm—spirituality and science. In terms of spirituality, many religious-philosophies (such as Zen, Hinduism, and mystical Christianity) hold that all existence is a unified whole. We are One. The Ultimate Reality is an indivisible whole. In terms of science, modern physics has reached the same conclusions. The universe is a unified whole. All separations are secondary realities to the primary reality of unity and oneness.

16

The New Age manager understands that the whole organization includes both managers and employees in a unified system and that all humankind and all existence (including subatomic existence) forms the one totality.

The chief characteristics of the New Age manager include wisdom, perspective, compassion, humor, empathy, and the ability to lead by creating meaning and purpose. Most of all, the New Age Manager never forgets that—*Employees Are People Too.*

CHAPTER THREE

The Fundamentals of New Age Management

The Buddhist point of view takes the function of work to be at least threefold: to give a man a chance to utilize and develop his faculties; to enable him to overcome his ego-centredness by joining with other people in a common task; and to bring forth the goods and services needed for a becoming existence. Again, the consequences that flow from this view are endless. To organize work in such a manner that it becomes meaningless, boring, stultifying, or nerve-racking for the worker would be little short of criminal; it would indicate a greater concern with goods than with people, an evil lack of compassion, and a soul-destroying degree of attachment to the most primitive side of this worldly existence.
> —E. F. Schumacher, *Small Is Beautiful: Economics as if People Mattered*

Holistic

Since the total employee goes to work for a company, the company must serve the total human being.
> —Hickman/Silva, *Creating Excellence: Managing Corporate Culture, Strategy, and Change in the New Age*

The key aspect of New Age Management is a "holistic" approach to employees. Some people even refer to New Age Management as "Holistic Management" since this concept is central to the New Age philosophy of management. Simply put, this concept involves treating employees as whole people, not just an another unit of production. Any manager worth his weight in paper clips knows that people are an

19

organization's greatest resource. Yet, the traditional management approach views workers in a one dimensional manner. Workers are just another unit of production to them.

New Age Managers need to understand the wide variety of human needs. They must understand Maslow's hierarchy of needs involving the basic needs of food and water, the security needs, the social needs, the need for self-esteem, the need for purpose and meaning, and the need for self-actualization. They should understand Douglas McGregor's Theory X and Theory Y, and the importance of assumptions. They should understand Frederick Herzberg's concepts of dissatisfiers and motivators. Without a comprehensive understanding of human nature, a manager is virtually worthless—and many are. New Age Managers know that human beings have a variety of personal, social, physical, economic, intellectual, emotional, and spiritual needs. The successful employee is one who has his/her life in balance, and who has developed a process for satisfying this variety of needs. No employer is likely to be able to fully meet all these needs, but the effective organization must meet many of them and avoid putting impediments in the employee's way so that he/she can meet the remaining needs off duty.

Studies have found that if any significant need is not being met, the whole person will suffer. This results in less effectiveness on the job. This is easily illustrated by considering one of the most basic needs— sleep. The first few months after our daughter was born, a good night's sleep was a rarity. I arrived at work a near zombie. My effectiveness was drastically reduced. If I could have taken a brief nap during the day (an hour or less), I could have produced more work with higher quality in seven hours than I did in eight hours in my semi-conscious state. How many employers do you know who officially sanction a nap? In other countries they have the siesta, but in the United States such opportunities are rare indeed. Yet, the value of the nap should not be underestimated. Dr. Peter Hanson, an expert on stress, teaches a "Power Nap" technique to top executives.

I'm not specifically advocating official nap periods. Most of the time for most employers this would be downright stupid. Lack of sleep in most situations is the result of poor planning on the part of the employee. Yet there are periods of time, such as the period immediately after the arrival of a little bundle of joy, when a serious sleep shortage may occur even with diligent efforts to avoid it. This is just a simple example of how failure to meet a non-work related need directly impacts performance at work.

20

It is easy to understand how a shortage of sleep impacts work. It is less obvious how the failure to meet other needs impacts work performance. For example, an employee who is not meeting her/his needs for love, sex, exercise, spiritual growth, family/community, fun/enjoyment, creativity, or self-fulfillment will likely suffer in work performance.

Again, this is not to say that managers must meet all these needs, but managers must understand that employees are whole people with many needs and must manage accordingly to be effective. A manager cannot afford to totally ignore all these other needs in establishing personnel and office policies. In setting office procedures and in managing people on a day-to-day basis, the manager must remember that the employee is a complex human being with a variety of needs, and if the manager hinders rather than assists an employee in maintaining his life in balance, the manager will fail to achieve maximum performance from that employee.

The New Age Manager will try to create a work environment which helps employees maintain a balanced life. This manager will not require an employee to travel on business so often that the absences begin to undermine the employee's family life, or move so often that it undermines the employee's sense of community. In making decisions, the New Age Manager always remembers that he/she is making decisions affecting a whole human being.

The traditionalist manager treats employees as just another unit of production. This manager does not consider the human aspects of the employee. This manager effectively dehumanizes the worker and forgets that workers are people too. The New Age Manager knows that workers are whole human beings and treats them accordingly. This is the fundamental philosophical difference between New Age Management and traditional management.

POT-SHOTS NO. 2051.

WHAT, YOU TOO!

I THOUGHT
I WAS
THE ONLY ONE
WITH THOUGHTS
AND FEELINGS.

Ashleigh Brilliant

Fun

The economic demands of the information society together with the new values of the baby boom generation are fostering the "work should be fun" idea.
—Naisbitt/Aburdene, *Re-inventing the Corporation: Transforming Your Job and Your Company for the New Information Society*

Fun is one of the most important features of New Age Management. Few issues so clearly separate the New Agers from the traditionalists. New Agers feel that life should be fun and, since work consumes such a big chunk of life, work should be fun as well. Many traditionalists feel guilty about fun, even fun off-duty. They fear fun may be a sin and they are certain it has no place at the work site.

Many types of work are inherently boring, routine, and unpleasant. It is difficult to make this type of work fun. However, the traditionalists wouldn't make work fun, even if they could. Thus, what would be a very difficult task to begin with, becomes an impossible task when there is no motivation to even try. The New Age Manager must try to restructure jobs to minimize the boring, repetitive, routine, and unpleasant features and inject elements of fun, humor, creativity, entertainment, etc. Don't just think of fun as a peripheral activity or periodic distraction or release from the real work. It can be fun and enjoyable to do a good job when the job is properly structured. Fun should be an integral part of the work.

You can be reasonably certain you are dealing with a New Age Manager if he has a sign on his desk asking "Are We Having Fun Yet?" A traditionalist would never even think to ask the question.

I'VE EXPLORED AND REJECTED EVERY OTHER POSSIBILITY —

LIFE, AFTER ALL, MUST BE FOR HAVING FUN.

Ashleigh Brilliant
POT-SHOTS NO. 2402.

©ASHLEIGH BRILLIANT 1982.

Meaningful

The leader is an effective social architect to the extent that he can manage meaning.

—Bennis/Nanus, *Leaders*

© BRILLIANT ENTERPRISES 1973

POT-SHOTS NO.431

Ashleigh
Brilliant

IF ONLY
I COULD GET
THAT WONDERFUL FEELING
OF ACCOMPLISHMENT
WITHOUT
HAVING TO
ACCOMPLISH
ANYTHING.

People need to feel that what they are doing matters. Management must constantly remind employees of the importance of their jobs, and remind them of the "big picture" and how their work fits into the overall picture. For a job to be "meaningful," it need not necessarily involve major issues of great historical significance. However, the job must make sense to the person doing it. The worker must feel that the job is worth doing. In some manner, the job must reinforce the employee's self-image and cause the employee to feel good about being part of a larger process which is accomplishing something worth doing. In short, the job needs to provide a purpose, a mission, an opportunity to be heroic.

Several years ago I had a frustrating experience with a potential employer who had a totally different perspective on this issue. I had applied for a position with an environmental protection group in New York City. During my interview I expressed my commitment to the goals of this agency. Normally one would think a prospective employer would be pleased that a potential employee understood the employer's mission and objectives, and strongly and sincerely supported them.

However, I was specifically informed that the most negative factor against me was my very commitment to their program. They said they didn't want people who already knew and supported their programs. They feared such people may be "zealots." They preferred people who would look upon this position as "just another job" and take a detached, objective approach.

I can understand an organization's concern over hiring "zealots." No manager would want to try to keep track of dozens of "Ollie Norths" running here and there. However, no organization can achieve maximum efficiency with people who consider their work as "just a job." Employees must be committed to the organization's objectives. They must have a sense of mission in order to go the extra mile and achieve peak performance. Any organization that doesn't understand this and take effective action to provide such a purpose is resigning itself to mediocrity.

Positive Feedbackp

Nothing is more powerful than positive feedback.
—Peters/Waterman, *In Search of Excellence*

Many management theorists have argued that the primary job of the manager is to provide positive feedback to the employees doing the work. The importance of positive feedback cannot be overstated. A manager who is effective at providing sincere, positive feedback will need to do little else to be successful.

The lack of positive feedback is a major problem in most organizations today. In fact, the word "positive" could be deleted and the statement would still be true. Many organizations provide little feedback of any kind, positive or negative. Timely feedback is essential for an effective organization. "Benign neglect" is not a good strategy for managing employees.

Most employees in any large organization starve for lack of positive feedback. If you can learn to provide sincere and meaningful positive reinforcements to people with whom you work (including supervisors and peers as well as subordinates), then you may not have to do much of anything else at all. Mary Kay Ash, founder of Mary Kay Cosmetics, notes in her tapes and books on "People Management" that the main reason she pays her managers is for them to make their employees feel good about doing their work.

If a behavior is sufficiently reinforced and rewarded, people will not only tolerate extremely difficult working conditions, but will actually seek out those conditions. With sufficient positive feedback, people will accept danger, injuries, disruption of personal and family life, physical abuse, being knocked down, beaten up, etc. and keep coming back for more. Just consider football players, boxers, test pilots, etc. (Now, you probably do not have the ability to use fame and fortune as feedback factors, but then you probably are not asking your employees to submit to this same degree of danger and pain either.) Don't underestimate the value of positive feedback. Every time you "catch someone doing something right," reinforce the behavior. People will love to work for you.

POT-SHOTS NO. 1229.

I WISH I HAD MORE INCENTIVE

TO DO WHAT I KNOW IS RIGHT.

Ashleigh Brilliant

© BRILLIANT ENTERPRISES 1977.

POT-SHOTS NO. 667

LOCAL, REGIONAL,
AND NATIONAL
AUTHORITIES
ALL APPROVED IT,

BUT
I NEVER DID.

© BRILLIANT ENTERPRISES 1974.

Participatory Management

The consensus process involves the person who must carry out a decision in the creation of that decision.
—Lawrence M. Miller, *American Spirit*

The New Age organization has an open decision making process. There is a high degree of employee involvement. In the traditional organization, a handful of managers make the decisions with little or no input from the workers or even middle management. In the New Age organization, everyone from the bottom to the top is constantly involved in decision making. The distinctions between worker and manager are significantly reduced as the employees have much more responsibility. The New Age organization practices co-management and allows employees to be self-managed to the maximum extent feasible.

This is not to say that decisions are made democratically by popular vote or that every decision is delayed until every employee can provide input. In an emergency situation, the manager may have to make command decisions. There may not be time for consultation and consensus building. However, the progressive organization makes a major effort to have maximum participation in as many different types of decisions as possible, from day-to-day work flow to major policy issues. The organization utilizes the talents, abilities, and knowledge of all employees, and does not just rely upon the wisdom of the few at the top.

A corollary to participatory management is the decentralization of authority. If all decisions must be made at the top in national headquarters, it is very difficult to obtain meaningful input from the actual work site locations. However, if the installation managers have authority to make most decisions right on the spot, then it is much easier to get the meaningful participation of the workers. Thus, de-centralization and participatory management are complimentary processes in terms of both theory and practice.

If the top management of an organization does not trust its local managers with any real decision-making authority, then it is extremely unlikely to trust the actual workers either. Likewise, the local managers cannot share decision-making authority with employees if they don't really have any such authority themselves. Centralized decision-making is antithetical to participatory management. To get power to the people (the workers) we must first get some degree of meaningful power to the local managers.

Flexibility

> *Treating everyone the same communicates the message, "I don't care enough about you to find out what makes you unique."*
> —Hickman/Silva, *Creating Excellence*

The New Age Manager puts people ahead of procedures. If the rigid application of company policy would result in an injustice, then the manager finds a way around the policy. The effective manager knows when and how to make exceptions to general practices. Application of the concept of "reasonable accommodation," like that which involves modifying an organization's practices or work methods to allow a handicapped employee to be able to function successfully, should be applied to all employees.

Flextime, the practice of allowing employees to start work at different times each day, is becoming a common example of the flexible approach. Requiring everyone to start every day at one set time fit the factory environment of the industrial age, but this approach is unnecessarily rigid for the office environment of the information age. This is just one simple example. There are dozens of other practices where uniformity needs to give way to individual practices based upon individual needs and circumstances.

© BRILLIANT ENTERPRISES 1970

POT-SHOTS NO. 222

ALL PEOPLE ARE DIFFERENT. THAT'S WHY EVERYBODY SHOULD BE TREATED THE SAME.

Open, Honest Communications

It is this combined demand for more information at faster speeds that is now undermining the great vertical hierarchies so typical of bureaucracy.
—Alvin Toffler, *Future Shock*

Some have called our era the "Age of Communications." There is more communication going up, down, and all around the world now than at any time in recorded history. Information and communications are central to modern society and organizations. One approach to understanding the work environment is to consider an organization as a communications system. An organization that has open lines of communication with valid, honest information going up, down, and throughout the organization will be much more effective and a much better place to work than the organization that attempts to restrict the flow of information or distort and deceive. When top managers attempt to keep employees in the dark, employees tend to become distrustful. This undermines loyalty and cooperation. When employees and lower level supervisors attempt to keep top management in the dark by distorting what is actually happening at the work site, this causes top management to function in a world of illusion rather than the world of reality. As a result, disastrous decisions are made which may totally destroy the organization.

It is easy to understand the value and importance of open, honest communications and valid information. Yet, few organizations are able to function in this manner. Internal politics and power struggles frequently lead to each division in an organization attempting to distort statistics and information for the advancement of particular individuals or groups. Since knowledge is power, those organizations that do not believe in sharing power with all employees do not want to share information either. For these reasons, much intra-organization communication is worthless or misleading. Yet, in the long run, poor communication will undermine the entire organization. Restricting communication and distorting information are symptoms of short-range thinking which will be noted again below. The New Age Manager must avoid these stupid, short-sighted traps and constantly strive for an open communication's system with objective information.

It is also important to keep in mind that effective communication isn't just talking, it is also listening. The most helpful kinds of information are still useless if people don't "hear" it. Most people are familiar with the concept of "active listening." This is an important skill for all employees and managers. All employees/managers should receive training in this area. One excellent self-study guide in this area is *Listening: The Forgotten Skill* by Madelyn Barley-Allen. A good listener is as important to effective communications as a good communicator.

POT-SHOTS NO. 1213.

COMMUNICATION WITH THE DEAD IS ONLY A LITTLE MORE DIFFICULT THAN COMMUNICATION WITH SOME OF THE LIVING.

POT-SHOTS NO. 2334.

HAVE PATIENCE:

ROME WAS NOT DESTROYED IN A DAY.

Three Dimensional Perspective

We have identified three basic attitude problems that most American executives suffer from today: short-term orientation, shallow thinking, and quick-fix expectations.
—Hickman/Silva, *Creating Excellence*

The traditional manager has a one dimensional view. He is very short-sighted. In making a decision, he only considers what is best for his particular work unit in the immediate future. He does not consider how his decision will impact other work units in the present and does not consider how his decision will impact his and other work units in the future. His decision has no depth and no width. Millions of these decisions are made every year and are a major cause of the decline of the American Economic Empire.

The New Age Manager is able to see beyond the immediate and beyond the obvious. The New Age Manager considers the broad impact of a decision. Understanding the universe to be a unified process or system, the New Age Manager knows that changing one thing sets off a ripple effect which will generate many other changes in many other places.

30

While the limits of human understanding make it impossible to fully anticipate the implications of every decision, the wise manager at least tries to anticipate as many of them as possible. In addition, just as the good manager must understand how a decision will spread out into space, he/she must understand how the decision will move out into time. He/she is not just interested in making decisions that look good today, but in decisions that will stand the test of time and maintain integrity in the future. This involves a high degree of patience. The good manager must cultivate patience and take the long range perspective. Three dimensional thinking is much more difficult than the "quick buck" approach, but for organizations to survive and prosper it is essential.

Minimal Use of Coercion

Learn to lead without coercion.
—John Heider, *The Tao of Leadership:*
Leadership Strategies for a New Age

© BRILLIANT ENTERPRISES 1977.

POT-SHOTS NO. 1323.

Ashleigh
Brilliant

DON'T BE NERVOUS —

JUST REMEMBER:

ALL MISTAKES WILL BE SEVERELY PUNISHED.

There are various types of power and many books written on the subject. The point here relates to negative power—or the process of getting employees to do what you want through punishment or the threat of punishment. This type of motivation can work in limited circumstances and is even necessary for certain individuals. However, most employees will not perform at their optimum level under the constant threat of punishment. The New Age Manager generally uses power as a last resort. He knows that rewards are a better motivator than punishments (the carrot always beats the stick) and that creating a situation where employees can grow and seek self-development and self-fulfillment is even more effective.

He also knows that there is always a side effect from the use of power. The use of power tends to generate an opposing reaction. An employee may comply with a direct order under threat of suspension or termination, but resentment and hostility will be the by-product. These negative emotions will almost inevitably result in some type of retaliation, active or passive, as the employee seeks to reassert his dignity. In an emergency situation, a manager may have no choice; but any manager who regularly relies upon threats of punishment as the primary means of gaining compliance with his direction will eventually undermine his authority and the work unit will become a virtual battle zone.

Minimal Layers of Management

America has too many managers and not enough leaders. If we had more leaders we would do without half of the managers.
—Bennis/Nanus, *Leaders*

© BRILLIANT ENTERPRISES 1975

POT-SHOTS NO. 858

THE CHIEF PURPOSE OF OUR ORGANIZATION IS TO PERPETUATE OUR ORGANIZATION.

Ashleigh Brilliant

When you begin with the assumptions that people are incapable of self-management, that they must be "managed" by others, you tend to create an organization with excessive numbers of managers and excessive layers of management. Even the lower level managers can't be trusted, so you have several layers of middle managers, who can't be trusted, and you have several layers of upper managers watching them. However, if you begin with a more realistic set of assumptions, and assume that employees are capable of a high degree of self-management and that first line supervisors can handle the facilitation of decision making at the production level, then multiple layers of management are not needed and can be seen as the liability that they truly are.

Virtually every organization has too many levels of managers, and reducing these layers is one of the essential steps in improving productivity and employee morale. Many of these excess managers serve no legitimate purpose. It would be wasteful enough if they just sat in their offices and read the newspapers all day, but most of them compound the waste by insisting on meddling with the work of the organization and thereby lowering productivity further. Every tiny, little, trivial "Mickey Mouse" problem or decision must be run by all these excess managers. Bad decisions are made worse and good decisions get watered down. The workers and line supervisors lose all say in the running of day-to-day operations as even minor matters require the approval of three layers of managers. When an organization has the time to over-manage to this extent, there are far too many managers.

It is impossible to provide absolute guidelines for the proper numbers of managers for all different types of organizations. However, a good rule of thumb would be no more than two levels of management between the first line supervisors and the head of a particular installation, or no more than four layers of managers at any work location. Many organizations have six to eight. Less than four would be better yet and should be the norm for a small work unit of less than 1,000 employees. There should be no more than one additional layer between the installation head and the very top manager in the whole organization.

Managers in this streamlined organization will obviously need deputies and assistants to help them with this scope of responsibility, but the layers of management will still be drastically reduced.

The biggest argument against reducing the layers of managers is that it eliminates promotional opportunities, and if good workers can't be promoted into higher levels of management and earn more money, they will leave the organization. This argument has an element of validity but is based on conflicting assumptions. Good employees do want more responsibility, challenges, and money. However, this can be provided without promoting people into duplicative management positions. Give good employees more responsibility and more money for doing meaningful work right where they are, rather than promote them into a do-nothing job.

Equalitarian

Most important for team building and effective team functioning is the leaders' success in reducing any status barriers between themselves and their subordinates.
—Dr. Thomas Gordon, *Leader Effective Training*

POT- SHOTS NO. 1313.

BE CAREFUL,

OR YOU'LL FALL

INTO

A

CATEGORY!

Ashleigh Brilliant

© BRILLIANT ENTERPRISES 1977.

The New Age organization seeks to minimize barriers between managers and employees, and reduce unnecessary status symbols and perks. This is not to say all perks should be eliminated. Perks can be effective motivators. An old Chinese expression notes something to the effect of "Why should I work hard to get ahead if still I'm going to be treated like everyone else?" While the New Age organization should try to treat all employees well, some employees will still be treated better. Plus, some status symbols are functional as well. Priority parking spaces are status symbols but are also functional for those who must use their cars during the day. Private offices are essential for those who must hold confidential meetings. The point here is not to treat every one exactly the same. This would be impossible and stupid even to try. The objective is to eliminate unnecessary and pretentious types of status symbols and perks that tend to divide people within an organization. Things such as "executive wash rooms" and special cafeterias for top staff are good examples of superfluous and unnecessary barriers. The real objective is to remove artificial distinctions that foster the "us versus them" mentality, and in its place create a sense of community, a sense of "we."

Developmental

The Baby Boomers of today, who constitute 48 percent of the work force, are vastly different from the work force of forty years ago. . . . They do not respond to dictatorial managers or leaders but are far more responsive to those leaders whom they perceive as having an interest in their personal growth and development.
—Zig Ziglar, *Top Performance*

The New Age organization is dedicated to helping its employees grow. This is a key element of long range planning and the three dimensional perspective noted above. For example, you have an excellent employee who does a good job for you. Then, there is an opportunity to send someone on a special project or assignment which would help develop the employee and assist the organization but has the short term effect of hurting your own work unit. This is a difficult decision for the manager. The short sighted approach is to keep the employee in your unit. The long range approach is to send the employee on the special assignment.

35

Managers who get a reputation of trying to hold their employees back will suffer in the long run because good employees will not want to work for them, whereas managers who get a reputation for supporting their employees, helping them grow and get ahead, will attract the top employees. This is true of entire organizations as well as individual units and managers within organizations.

The special assignment situation should be a fairly easy decision. The employee is only gone for a short time and then returns. Providing growth on the job by giving additional responsibilities, providing training, and allowing more self-management are other ways of developing employees, and are also relatively easy decisions to make. Promotions present a more difficult issue because they generally involve losing the good employee permanently. Yet, good managers must help good employees advance or good employees will avoid their units. An organization can only grow and become more effective when its employees are growing and becoming more effective.

Ashleigh Brilliant

POT-SHOTS NO. 1296.

WOULDN'T IT BE NICE IF I COULD FULFIL MY DESTINY BY HELPING YOU FULFIL YOURS.

© BRILLIANT ENTERPRISES 1977.

Positive Orientation to Change

*If we had to choose one essential characteristic of what we call the
New Age, that characteristic would be change.*
—Hickman/Silva, *Creating Excellence*

Some have called our times the "Age of Change." Rapid change
has become a primary fact of life for almost all organizations. There is
little that can be done to alter this fact. However, organizations can
choose various attitudes towards this fact. An organization can seek to
resist or ignore change. (American auto companies took this approach
for several years until they almost went bankrupt.) Or an organization
can welcome change, try to anticipate future trends, and be prepared to
move with the times.

This is a major difference between the traditionalist approach and
the New Age philosophy. New Agers are future-oriented. Traditionalists are oriented to the past. The traditionalists are so fond of the
old ways of doing things that they are afraid of change, and resist or
ignore it until they are overwhelmed by it. The New Agers love change.
They want more change to have more progress. Even today's rapid rate
of change is too slow for some New Agers. They are constantly devising
plans to speed up the change. Since more and faster change appears to
be the trend, whether one likes it or not, the New Agers' orientation is
much more positive and in tune with the emerging reality.

An organization with a positive view of change creates a natural
system rather than a mechanical system. A natural organizational
structure is capable of continuous change and growth; a mechanical
structure is a fixed entity that just does the same thing over and over. A
mechanical system must be perfect or it will not work; a natural system
can tolerate imperfections because it is capable of self-adjustment.
Even if a perfect mechanical system is initially constructed, when the
external environment changes it becomes obsolete; a natural system
can more quickly adapt to the inevitable external changes. The more
easily an organization can adapt to change (internal and external) the
more natural it is, and the greater its chances of long term success and
survival.

© BRILLIANT ENTERPRISES 1975.

THERE HAS BEEN AN ALARMING INCREASE

IN THE NUMBER OF THINGS

I KNOW NOTHING ABOUT.

Ashleigh Brilliant

Three Exercises in Applying the Fundamentals

The following three quick exercises are designed to generate some specific ideas which you can use at present in your organization.

New Age or Traditionalist?

Following each of the concepts below, check "T" for those you feel are traditionalist approaches and check "N" for those you think reflect the New Age Philosophy. There are no "right" answers listed. Most of the answers are actually rather obvious. This one is just to get you thinking and applying the general concepts to specific practices. Try it.

NT

☐☐	*Company Sponsored Day Care*
☐☐	*Open Door Policy (Where any employee in an organization has direct access and an opportunity to talk to the top managers)*
☐☐	*Recreational Facilities On-Site*
☐☐	*Exercise Facilities On-Site*
☐☐	*Use of Questionnaires to Obtain Employee Input*
☐☐	*Quality Circles*
☐☐	*Brainstorming Sessions*
☐☐	*Managers as Cops*
☐☐	*Halloween Costume Contest*
☐☐	*Suggestion Boxes*
☐☐	*Banning Plants and Posters from the Work Areas*

Internal Brainstorming

Now that you have given some thought to specific practices, let's begin to apply the general concepts to your own organization. Below I have listed the 13 (unlucky 13 for traditionalists) major concepts of New Age Management. After each concept is a place for five specific applications. Thinking about your own organization, try to list five specific ideas related to the general concept which could conceivably apply to your work environment. This is a brainstorming approach, so don't worry about whether a particular idea is good or bad or realistic at this point. We will evaluate the ideas later. The goal here is just to generate at least five specific ideas for your own work environment. If you can get more than five, that's great. But try to get at least five.

Again, don't be afraid to be outrageous. These ideas do not have to be realistic or perfectly thought out. You will analyze and perfect the ideas in the final step.

For example, here are a few extreme ideas under the "holistic" concept to give you an idea of what the boundaries are (or aren't) at this point in the process.

On-Site Auto Mechanics Since almost all employees need car service, and since getting a car serviced is time consuming, expensive, and subjects the employee to a high risk of rip-offs, the company could provide on-site auto service. This would be convenient, fair, and reputable. Again, I'm not actually recommending this idea to anyone, just listing an unusual idea to help get you going.

Lovers' Lounge Since any organization with people with compatible sexual orientations (in the old days one would have just said opposite sexes, but these days gender is less important than sexual orientation) is likely to have some office romances or office liaisons, the organization could provide handy dandy on-site lovers' lounges for some quick afternoon delight rather than forcing your employees to sneak out over lunch and risk getting flea poisoning at some cheap rent-by-the-minute motel. One more time, I'm not actually recommending this, just demonstrating the wide range of ideas that can be generated if you take a holistic approach to employees and start thinking of ways to help meet all their needs. This particular idea seems rather unlikely to be accepted in America. It seems more suited for France or Sweden. (Maybe I'll send a few resumes to Swedish companies???.)

Financial Planning Services, Barbers/Hair Stylists, Postal Services, Meditation Rooms, etc.

OK, now you have the idea. Try applying the concepts to your organization.

A. *Holistic*
   1. _____
   2. _____
   3. _____
   4. _____
   5. _____

B. *Fun*
   1. _____
   2. _____
   3. _____
   4. _____
   5. _____

C. *Meaningful*
   1. _____
   2. _____
   3. _____
   4. _____
   5. _____

D. *Positive Feedback*
   1. _____
   2. _____
   3. _____
   4. _____
   5. _____

E. *Participatory Management*
   1. _____
   2. _____
   3. _____
   4. _____
   5. _____

F. *Flexibility*
   1. _____
   2. _____
   3. _____
   4. _____
   5. _____

G. *Open, Honest Communications*
    1. _____
    2. _____
    3. _____
    4. _____
    5. _____

H. *Three Dimensional Perspective*
    1. _____
    2. _____
    3. _____
    4. _____
    5. _____

I. *Minimal Use of Coercion*
    1. _____
    2. _____
    3. _____
    4. _____
    5. _____

J. *Minimal Layers of Management*
    1. _____
    2. _____
    3. _____
    4. _____
    5. _____

K. *Equalitarian*
    1. _____
    2. _____
    3. _____
    4. _____
    5. _____

L. *Developmental*
    1. _____
    2. _____
    3. _____
    4. _____
    5. _____

M. *Positive Orientation to Change*
   1. _____
   2. _____
   3. _____
   4. _____
   5. _____

Refinement and Analysis

Now you should have a few dozen ideas for your organization. Go back over them and review each one. Circle the one idea in each group that appears most realistic and most likely to help your organization. Then, think it through and fill in the details. Modify it as needed.

After you have done this, you should have 13 ideas which are within the bounds of reason and which would help your organization. Now, recognize that you can't change everything at once. So review your top 13 ideas and select the one that would be the easiest for you to implement. This may not be the best idea on your list or the one that would help your organization the most, but you want to start with something that can be done. If your greatest idea would require approval from 800 middle managers and take six years to implement, this is not the place to start. So find your easiest idea to implement and go to it.

Once you have successfully implemented this one idea, come back to your list and take the next easiest idea to implement and proceed accordingly. Great ideas mean nothing unless they can be effectuated. As you practice implementing your easier ideas, you will gain insight and skills into getting things done in your organization. This will lay the foundation for getting your great ideas implemented later on.

CHAPTER FOUR

Working in the New Age

In the new paradigm, work is a vehicle for transformation.
—Marilyn Ferguson, *The Aquarian Conspiracy*

We have considered work from the standpoint of management. Now, let's examine work from the viewpoint of the worker. Remember that all employees are workers, including managers, so this chapter is relevant for both workers and managers.

Is Work a Four-Letter Word?

Most men would feel insulted if it were proposed to employ them in throwing stones over a wall, and then in throwing them back, merely that they might earn their wages. But many are no more worthily employed now.
—Henry David Thoreau

During the industrial age, work was so dehumanized that the word "work" became the ultimate four-letter word to many people. Like Maynard on the old Dobie Gillis TV show, most people had an immediate, negative reaction to the word. Work was, at best, a necessary evil. Workers lived for quitting time and the weekend. "Thank God It's Friday" was a sincere expression.

Unfortunately, many people still look at work this way. If one works for a New Age organization, there is no one to blame but the employee. The employee needs a change of perspective. If one works for a traditionalist organization, the negative view of work is more understandable, but no more acceptable. Work is a huge chunk of one's life. It is a waste of one's life and one's energy to spend that much time

45

at something one dislikes. Employees must take responsibility for their lives and make the necessary changes to create positive work situations. This may require a change in jobs or companies, or may just require a new attitude towards one's current job.

The point is; if you dislike what you are doing then it is unlikely you will do it very well. This is unfair to the employer and unfair to yourself. You must seek to change such a situation.

Right Livelihood

The word "livelihood" is a good way to describe our employment, for our work should be alive and vital to us. If it is not, we are probably in the wrong line of business.
—Margaret R. Stortz, *Start Living Every Day of Your Life*

Just as the first fundamental for the New Age Manager involves the "holistic" approach, this is eqully true for the New Age Worker. Employees need to understand that their happiness and well-being require a holistic approach which involves meeting all their needs. The whole employee must deal with the same range of needs as the whole manager. Both are people who must meet the entire scope of human needs. The employee must meet the needs of the body for sleep, exercise, food, sex, etc; the needs of the mind for accomplishments, development, understanding, meaning, creativity, etc; the needs of the emotions for love, community, friendship, family, etc; and the needs of the spirit for unity with something beyond the purely physical. Great success in one area will not fully compensate for failure to meet other needs. Any unmet need will have an adverse impact upon the entire person. Having the "right" job is an important part of getting one's life in balance.

The concept of "right livelihood" comes from the Buddha's Eightfold Path and is one of the steps to enlightenment. The "right" job meets (or is at least complimentary to) the needs of the body, mind, emotions, and spirit. If you don't feel your present job is the "right" one, there are essentially three options: change jobs, change the job you have to make it better, or change you attitude towards your job. You must do one of these three things. To continue to work for a long period of time in a job that you feel is not "right" for you will ultimately undermine your spirit and your life. We will consider each of these three options further on—changing your current job (Job Tailoring), changing jobs (The Great Escape), and changing your attitude towards your job (Transforming Work).

Career Objectives: What Do You Want To Be Now That You Are All Grown Up?

Many people have realized over the past decade that they took the wrong career road and have started reexamining their career objectives. *What Color Is Your Parachute? A Practical Manual for Job-Hunters and Career Changers* by Richard Bolles, and *Wishcraft: How to Get What You Really Want* by Barbara Sher and Anne Gottlieb, are excellent books designed to help people examine what they really want to do. If you are still stuck in this space, not knowing what your objectives really are, then please check out one of these books. It's been said many times, many ways, but is still true that you have to know what you want in order to get it. Determining your objectives is the first step. Until you know exactly what you want, you can't intelligently choose from among the three options noted above.

In considering your objectives, you want to be able to answer several questions. What do I want right now? What do I want to be doing in a year? What do I want to be doing in five years? What do I want to accomplish before I retire? And most importantly, what do I want to accomplish before I die? In short, you need to discover your life's misison and develop a strategy for achieving it.

POT-SHOTS NO. 556

Ashleigh
Brilliant

MY OBJECT IS
TO SAVE
THE WORLD,

WHILE
STILL LEADING
A PLEASANT LIFE.

© BRILLIANT ENTERPRISES 1974.

Skills Analysis

In addition to understanding your "purpose," there are two other key elements to the "right" job. One involves utilizing your best skills, and the other involves being happy with the people you work with. We will first discuss skills. You are better at some things than others. The key to success and happiness is to get a job that allows you to use your best skills. Once you get such a job, don't allow yourself to be promoted out of it into a job where you can't use your best skills. The extra money will never offset the lack of satisfaction. We have all seen good workers take one promotion too many and become living examples of the Peter Principle. For example, if you are a great teacher, but a poor supervisor, don't take that administrative job, stay in the class room. The extra money from the promotion will not offset the loss in self-satisfaction from using your best skills and working at your maximum effectiveness. If you don't know what your best skills are, then do the following exercises. (For a much more detailed and elaborate skills analysis, examine the exercises in *What Color is Your Parachute?*)

After each skill listed below, indicate your self-appraisal from "A" (something you are very good at) to "F" (something you can't do well at all).

Machine or Manual: *Training Others:*
Athletic: *Briefing:*
Memory: *Consulting/Advising:*
Numerical: *Creative/Imaginative:*
Financial: *Artistic:*
Influencing/Persuading: *Listening:*
Performing: *Perceptive:*
Planning/Organizing: *Intelligence:*
Judging Other's Effectiveness: *Common Sense:*
Getting Others to Work: *Researching:*
Reading and Comprehending: *Interviewing:*
Writing: *Problem-Solving:*
Oral Communications: *Others:*
Public Speaking:

Do your skills match your objectives? If your objective is to be President of the United States and you can't use mass media (like Walter Mondale), then you had best find a new objective.

©BRILLIANT ENTERPRISES 1977 POT-SHOTS NO. 1266.
IF ONLY OUR GREAT THINKERS COULD LEARN TO TALK, AND OUR GREAT TALKERS COULD LEARN TO THINK!
Ashleigh Brilliant

People As Environment

A critical factor in liking your work is people. Your job environment isn't just furniture, space, rules, systems, and procedures: it's made up of people as well. How you feel about your physical environment and the rules and systems affecting your job depends in large part on how you feel about your people environment. Your relationships with people are the key to liking your work.
—from Working and Liking It

An important part of finding the "right" job is finding the "right" people to work with. Many workers ignore this fact. They think in terms of their skills (properly so), the status of the job, the pay, the perks, the location, the commute, etc. However, they often neglect to consider whether they will fit in with the other people in the organization, i.e. do you prefer working with intellectuals? introverts? extroverts? etc.

I won't belabor this point, but it is important. In setting your objectives you must take the people environment into account. No matter how great a job you get, if you don't like the people you work with, you will probably grow to dislike the job.

The Ultimate Question

If you have a job at present, review your objectives, skills, and desired people environment and ask yourself this question: Is there a better job for me somewhere else? If yes, go get it. If no, thank your lucky stars (and your employer) that you already have the best possible job for you in the whole wide world.

Is this too simple? Perhaps you like your job, but it could be better. They could all be better. How about "job tailoring"?

Job Tailoring

Once you have developed your objectives and have more than a vague idea of what you want from a job, then you should evaluate your current job in terms of how well or how poorly that job meets your objectives. The ultimate decision you must make is whether to stay with your current job or seek a new one. It is at this point that many people jump from the frying pan into the fire. Don't quit your current job unless you have performed a job tailoring analysis and decided the job has so many more negatives than positives that there is no way to save it. For many people it may be easier to tailor their existing job into one they would like than to start fresh with something totally different. The first step in determining whether your job can be "tailored" into one you would like better is to do a job tailoring analysis.

This simply involves setting up a chart as follows:

Things I Like About My Job	Things I Dislike About My Job

List everything you can possibly think of under each item, no matter how large or trivial. If you have allowed negativism to overwhelm you, your initial reaction may be, "There is nothing good about my job." But this is bunk. If there was nothing good about your job at all, you wouldn't do it. You are not a slave. You have a choice. They must pay you. Even if it's not as much as you would like, they still pay you. So that is one positive. You must have some benefits, you must enjoy talking to some of your co-workers, etc. List everything pro and con. The following is a hypothetical example:

Things I Like About My Job	Things I Dislike About My Job
Getting Paid	*Long Commute*
Attractive Secretary	*Difficult Parking*
Across from Nieman-Marcus	*Substandard Office Machines*
Free Baseball Game Tickets	*No Fast Food in Area*
Nice Office	*Long Useless Monthly Reports*
Good Retirement System	*Too Much Travel*
Stock Options	*Not Enough Members of Opposite Sex*
Vacations	*Company VP Hates Me for Seducing*
Can Live in San Francisco	*Budget Manager's Spouse, Will Try*
Free Daily Newspaper	*to Block Future Promotions*
Like Boss	*Briefing Major Stockholders*
Like Co-Workers	
Get to Teach Often	
Get to Write Newsletter	

After preparing your own lists, analyze the likes and dislikes. You may well find that there is a lot more about your job that you like than you generally realize. In any event, you weigh the pros and cons, and decide whether the job is worth trying to tailor. If there are a lot of good points, then look at the bad points. Are there ways to reduce or eliminate them? Are there ways to increase the positive features? Don't expect to get rid of all the bad points, but if you can reduce them and increase the positive, then your tailored job may be just right for you. For example, your job may involve three major functions. Perhaps you like two of them and dislike the third. There may be a way for you to be able to concentrate your efforts in the areas you enjoy.

If your current job is a loser, then the next logical step is to consider other jobs within your current organization. Perhaps there are promotional opportunities into jobs more to your liking. If not, consider reassignment or even voluntary demotions to find something more appropriate to your needs. Don't get hung up on status symbols and feel you must hang on to a higher level job when a lower level job would suit your overall needs better. If there are no realistic alternatives within your organization, then you may have to take the big plunge.

The Great Escape

Quitting an organization, especially one you have been with for a long time, requires a lot of courage. It is not a decision one should take lightly. However, if there is no way to tailor your job into something acceptable and there are no alternative positions available in your organization, then you have little choice. To stay with a job that makes you unhappy will throw your life out of balance. Your unhappiness at work will spill over into other areas of your life. If you can't fit in, leave. Remember there are always options. All the options may appear bad and it may seem to be a choice among the lesser of various evils, but there are options. Try something new. The worse option is to do nothing.

POT-SHOTS NO. 1069.

IF YOU CAN'T BEAT THEM OR JOIN THEM,

Ashleigh Brilliant

TRY TO GET AWAY FROM THEM.

Transforming Work

Paying attention is the essence of true spirituality. When we pay attention, whatever we are doing is transformed and becomes a part of our spiritual path.
—from *Chop Wood, Carry Water, A Guide to Finding Spiritual Fulfillment in Everyday Life*

All workers must perform some unpleasant tasks. There is no "perfect" job. Even ballet dancers, basketball stars, and actors must spend many tedious hours practicing for the few hours in the limelight. So whether you have a great job with a few undesirable duties or a terrible job with many unpleasant functions, the following techniques for transforming work may be helpful. By transforming work, I mean the ability to turn generally boring, routine, and unpleasant duties into something positive and personally rewarding. These concepts can be used for household chores as well as work assignments.

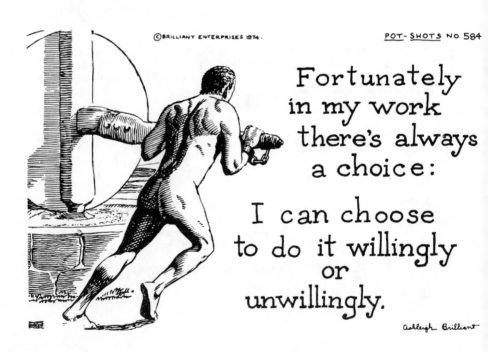

©BRILLIANT ENTERPRISES 1974.

POT-SHOTS NO. 584

Fortunately in my work there's always a choice:

I can choose to do it willingly or unwillingly.

Ashleigh Brilliant

Quality Work as a Commitment to Self

> *Furthermore, we may state that the chief purpose of work is not to produce things but to build the man. . . . It is not so important what shape or form our work may take; what is vitally important is our attitude towards that work.*
> —Edmond Szekely, *Creative Work: Karma Yoga*

The key to transforming work is a commitment to quality. Even if the particular duty is one which doesn't seem worth doing, if you must do it, it is important to do it right. Even if no one else will ever know whether you did it right or not, *you will know.* By making a commitment to quality work, you make a commitment to yourself to develop your abilities, self-respect, and self-discipline, to do the best you can do and be the best you can be. When you do as little as possible or just enough to get by, you are not merely cheating your employer, your customers, your clients, and your co-workers, but most importantly, you cheat yourself. You cheat yourself out of an opportunity to develop pride and self-worth. You cheat yourself out of an opportunity to meet a challenge and develop your own inner powers and abilities. You may be able to get away with cheating others, but you never get away with cheating yourself.

Thus, the key to transforming work is a commitment to yourself to use every possible opportunity for self-development and treat every work assignment, no matter how small or boring, as a challenge that can be used in your development.

Work as Meditation

> *Work can be a deeply enriching—and meditative—experience. It all depends on the attitude we carry to it. Approaching work with care and awareness can transform even the most mundane task into an exciting opportunity to reflect and grow.*
> —from *Chop Wood, Carry Water*

Another effective way to transform dull or repetitive work is to treat the work as a meditation session. There are an infinite variety of meditation methods. The essence of virtually all meditation techniques is concentration, attention, the ability to focus totally on just one thing at a time. It doesn't make much difference what you choose to meditate upon. It can be your own breathing process, a candle flame, a word (mantra), etc. It is your ability to channel your conscious attention upon one single area that is the key to effective meditation.

Many daily duties are suitable for meditation. This includes activities from filing papers to typing a letter to peeling carrots to commuting to work. (How often do you pay full attention to your driving? Do you ever turn off the radio, stop all discussions, stop your mind from darting about and just focus all your efforts on driving? I don't do this very often either, just when my tape deck is broken, but it does present a real opportunity for meditation while improving your driving.) The more routine and repetitious the activity is, the better suited it is for this type of meditation. The key is your consciousness. Focus entirely upon what you are doing. Precisely what you are doing is secondary. It is the ability to focus your full attention on the activity that is central. Become what you are doing, think of nothing else. If your mind starts to roam, and it will, just gently bring it back to the task at hand.

Even if you are required to do the most nonsensical type of work (such as the classic military assignment of digging a hole and then filling it back up and then digging it again and filling it again on and on, or if like Sisyphus you must push a stone to the top of the hill only to have it roll back down and have to push it up again over and over), you can transform the work from a meaningless exercise into a meaningful meditation.

Before leaving this item, just a quick note on meditation. Some people erroneously assume that meditating is just for people who believe in various Eastern religious-philosophies. This is not true. Today, progressive Christian, Jewish, and Moslem groups (as well as non-religious groups) are discovering the value and validity of meditation. So don't discard this idea just because you aren't a Zen Buddhist.

POT-SHOTS NO. 759

I don't have any solution, but I certainly admire the problem.

aahleigh Brilliant

Work as a Projection of Self

> *Consciousness can regard any job as a potential opportunity for self-expression, for play, for creativity, for the furtherance of social objectives, and it can arrange the factors in the job so that they form a means of self-expression.*
> —Charles Reich, *The Greening of America*

Most jobs contain at least some limited options for creativity. To the extent that any job can be done in different ways, the job presents you with an opportunity to project your unique abilities and values into that job. Any type of communication, written or oral, presents a significant opportunity for creative expression. Even if your efforts are reviewed and must be toned down to fit into the mold of your organization, there is always a slight crack through which you can project your unique personality. Use these opportunities to express and confirm your existence.

Work as Service

> *How does a person obtain a better position and increased income? The person whose thought is upon service is certain to glorify even the most insignificant position.*
> —Frank Whitney, *Foundations of Unity: A Source Book of the Church of Unity*

If you have contact with other people, either customers or coworkers, you can use your job as an opportunity to serve others. It is very rewarding to be able to help people. For example, if you are a waiter/waitress, you can turn what seems to be awful job into an opportunity to help people. We have all seen waiters who clearly hate their jobs and provide minimal service (and hopefully get minimal tips). On the other hand, we have all seen waiters who go beyond the expected and are genuinely helpful, pleasant, and considerate (not overbearing, pretentious, or chatterboxes) but sincerely interested in serving you.

Where I work we have an outstanding security guard. He sits at the front desk and makes sure everyone entering the building has a badge and that no one sneaks in and blows up our computer system. This is not what I would consider to be a fun job. But he has literally transformed this job into a true service. Unlike many other guards who wouldn't say "hello" without a requirement in their contract mandating it, this guard always has a cheerful "good morning" and is extremely creative at finding ways to assist people. He is a pleasure to see and talk to. He provides concrete evidence that any job can be transformed.

Mother Teresa teaches people to see the human needs right in front of them. It is not necessary to have a powerful position to help people. Start from where you are. We are all surrounded by opportunities to assist others. As William Blake said, "If one is to do good, one must do it in the minute particulars."

Enlightened Workers as Social Revolutionaries

> Work also becomes a medium through which the individual can express the vision of the Aquarian Conspiracy.
> —Marilyn Ferguson, *The Aquarian Conspiracy*

©ASHLEIGH BRILLIANT 1981.

POT-SHOTS NO. 2265.

MAKE YOURSELF USEFUL TO YOUR OPPRESSORS,

UNTIL YOU'RE STRONG ENOUGH TO OVERTHROW THEM.

Ashleigh Brilliant

Earlier I had a section on managers as social revolutionaries. While workers have less ability to change the social system that makes up the work environment, workers can have an impact. With less power and less formal responsibility in this area, a worker frequently must be careful and subtle in seeking social change. However, the clever worker can seek ways to influence the system and create a more positive work environment. You just have to do what you can do from where you are. It may not seem like much but with millions of workers (including managers) sharing your desire to implement a progressive philosophy in the work environment every little step helps bring your organization closer to the New Age. Explore every assignment for potential to insert a little sunshine into your organization. A few rays here, a few rays there, and next thing you know, your organization is moving out of the darkness of the traditionalist/industrial era into the light of the New Age.

CHAPTER FIVE

Ten Keys to Success: How to Achieve Your Career Objectives

Whatever your objectives (promotions, reassignment, relocation, awards, job restructuring, transfer, better desk, bigger office, avoiding a demotion, etc), there are some common factors which will increase your chances of success. Most of these are perfectly obvious and yet they are overlooked all the time with disastrous results.

Positive Attitude

The greatest discovery of any generation is that human beings can alter their lives by altering their attitudes of mind.
—Albert Schweitzer

Over 35 years ago Norman Vincent Peale wrote a book called *The Power of Positive Thinking* which went on to become one of the greatest selling books of all time, selling over seven million copies. (My book should be so blessed.) Since then, the concepts of positive thinking and positive attitudes have become something of a cliche and many people now pay the idea little mind. Yet positive thinking does work.

The concept was already ancient when Dr. Peale popularized it. The concept is found in the Bible and other holy books from East and West alike. Various religious groups have made positive thinking a cornerstone of their religious practices, involving prayer, meditation, and affirmations. Modern examples of such religious groups include various "New Thought" Christian schools (New Thought oriented in

61

the 1800's) such as the Church of Unity and Church of Religious Science.

The power of our thoughts to create our reality is a common theme in New Age literature. Several scientific research projects have also reached the conclusion that the way we think determines to a great extent what we experience. One would have to be a fool to overlook the importance of using positive thinking for you rather than allowing negative thinking to work against you.

In recent years, research in psychopharmacology has proven what many people have known over the centuries; a positive attitude is good for you, good for your health, good for your wealth, good for everything. Researchers found that a positive attitude produces a specific chemical reaction which makes people feel better, while negative thinking results in a decline of endorphins and shuts down the immune system. This leads to illness and depression. Positive thoughts will make you feel better. Even if you must begin by literally forcing yourself to be positive (faking it, so to speak), it will become contagious and the positive thoughts will generate nice little chemicals and good feelings which will reinforce the positive thoughts.

For example, if you force yourself to smile or laugh, even when you don't feel like smiling or laughing, if you keep at it for a few minutes, you will soon feel like it. Feelings can generate thoughts, but thoughts can also generate feelings. Control your thoughts and you can control your feelings.

Positive thinking is important in all aspects of our lives, including work. There is probably no single factor more important in determining your success in achieving your career objectives than your own attitude. While a positive attitude alone will not absolutely guarantee success, a negative attitude will guarantee failure.

It's often been said that in the land of the blind, the one-eyed man is king. And in the office of militant negativism, the positive employee shines like gold. The good news is that this vital key to success is totally within your control. Use it.

You cannot control external events, but you can learn to control your reaction to those events and thereby have a positive attitude and be happy. There are numerous techniques and approaches to learning to control our internal reactions to external events. Virtually every major religion and many minor religions are almost totally founded upon their own specific technique. Plus, there are numerous secular methods as well. EST is one example. Whether the underlying philosophy is Christian, Buddhist, secular, or something else, almost all the methods will work if properly and persistently applied. In fact, it is relatively easy to devise your own techniques once you understand the goal and the process.

One of my favorite approaches is the "Living Love Way to Happiness and Higher Consciousness" by Ken Keyes, Jr. The following extended excerpt, which Mr. Keyes kindly allows others to use, is reprinted from his *Handbook to Higher Consciousness,* Fifth Edition, Copyright 1975 by the Living Love Center. (790 Commercial Ave. Coos Bay, OR, 97420)

"The Living Love Way to Happiness and Higher Consciousness" is a "Science of Happiness" which was formulated to contribute toward the great awakening now taking place throughout the world. . . .

As you work toward higher levels of consciousness, you will find that you have always had enough to be happy. It is the patterns in your head that make you unhappy, although you usually blame the people and conditions outside you for your unhappiness. . . .

And we always have enough to be happy if we are enjoying what we do have—and not worrying about what we don't have. . . .

The world tends to be your mirror. A peaceful person lives in a peaceful world. An angry person creates an angry world. A helpful person generates helpful, loving energy in others. An unfriendly person should not be surprised when he or she meets only people who sooner or later respond in an unfriendly way. A happy person finds the world filled with happy people. . . .

Your predictions and expectations are thus self-fulfilling. Since your consciousness creates your universe, all you have to do to change your world is to change your consciousness! . . .

You really savor living when you consciously experience everything that you feel and do as taking place in the theater that we call our world. You see yourself and others as actors in the daily drama of life. But the real you is not your body or mind. You're not the actor. The real you is your Conscious-awareness. . . .

In the fourth Center of Consciousness, you experience "work" as an expression of love and caring. "Work" is no longer performed unconsciously or mechanically with the feeling that one can fully enjoy life again when the job is done. You will increase your growth into higher consciousness by learning to flow energy into meeting the needs of "others" as though they were your own needs. . . .

You will also begin to deeply feel that you live in a perfect world. You will not feel it as perfect from the limited point of view of your instant happiness when you have addictive programming. But your world is perfect from the point of view of continually providing you with precisely the life experiences that you need for your overall development as a conscious being. . . .

You will discover that working on your consciousness is the most fulfilling thing you can do in your life. . . .

And you do this all the time in your busy life so that your entire life becomes a meditation. . . .

Since the outside realities are only minimally changeable by you, your happiness depends on your concentrating on changing what you can change—your emotional programming. . . .

The only effective and permanent way to change the world in which we live is to change our level of consciousness. . . ."

The key to success, happiness, and peace of mind is your own attitudes. The place to start the revolution is in your own mind with your own attitudes.

© BRILLIANT ENTERPRISES 1974   POT-SHOTS NO. 490

I DON'T KNOW HOW TO BE HAPPY—

They didn't teach it in my school.

Ashleigh Brilliant

Your Primary Job Duty is to Make Your Boss Happy

Most of your job activities should be directed to this vital success strategy—help your boss succeed.
—Andrew Dubrin, *Winning at Office Politics*

Your relationship with your supervisor is the most important relationship in the work environment. If you can establish a good working relationship with your boss, everything else will fall into place. This should be perfectly obvious, yet this is an area where many employees go astray. Rather than doing everything reasonable to help their bosses, they develop a confrontational attitude and try to undermine him/her. Rather than seeking to create an ally, they seek to create an enemy. This is the path to disaster. A good relationship with your boss means a more pleasant working environment and better career opportunities. A bad relationship means numerous daily hassles and very limited prospects for advancement.

This is not to say that an employee should kowtow, apple-polish, bootlick, or grovel to gain supervisory favors. Rather it means that the employee should do a good job and make a meaningful contribution to help the supervisor achieve his/her own objectives. You will note that in these "ten keys to success" there is not a separate item on "doing a good job." Doing a good job is part of making your boss happy. It is intentionally not listed as a separate item. It is hard to define exactly what doing a good job involves in many positions. You may think a "good job" involves doing something other than what your boss wants. If so, you have a serious problem. Your job is to help your boss accomplish their job. You are doing a good job when what you do helps them meet their goals.

Thus, the first step in establishing a good working relationship with your boss is to find out what your boss is trying to achieve. What are the goals and objectives of your boss? Are there production goals? Does your boss have certain personal objectives? One thing you can be sure about is that one of your supervisor's objectives will be to look good to their own manager. Anything you can do to help your boss look good to their boss will pay good dividends to you as well.

Frequently, what is really important to your boss is not clearly defined in your formal position duties at all. In these situations it may be necessary to modify the way you spend your time to put more energy into projects helpful to your boss, and less time on your officially designated duties. If you are specifically given duties outside your designated area, you could protest and complain and raise procedural objections. You might even win the battle, but you would likely lose the war. Fighting with your boss is totally self-defeating. Your job is to help your boss find ways to achieve his/her objectives, not to put impediments in their way.

Maybe you say that your boss is a total jerk (a real possibility especially in traditionally oriented organizations) and that there is no way you can establish a good, positive, cordial working relationship. If this is the case, you must either change your attitude or change your boss. There is simply no pay-off (unless you consider ulcers and terminations to be pay-offs) in fighting with your boss. If you can't get along with your manager, despite reasonable and conscientious efforts on your part, then you must find a way to get reassigned or transferred to another manager. You must find a manager that you can get along with in order to be effective. If all the managers in your organization are jerks (very unlikely), then quit and go elsewhere.

Having a good working relationship with your boss doesn't mean that you have to become personal friends. Friends are nice, but sometimes bosses don't share your outside interests and there is no basis for anything other than a work relationship. This is fine. It is the relationship at work that counts. Your boss needs to understand that you are doing your best to help her meet her objectives and that you expect she will likewise try and help you achieve your objectives. This doesn't mean you establish a formal *quid pro quo,* but your boss will know which employees are being truly helpful. There is a natural human tendency to like people who give us what we want and to help people we like.

Another bad situation you may find yourself in is where your boss has no objectives. Your boss has burned out and is just waiting to retire (even though retirement age may be 15 years in the future). Nothing you do can help or please them because nothing you do really matters to them. They may like you as a person but they aren't interested in your work or in helping you. Get away from this kind of person as quick as you can. It is not enough merely to avoid having a bad relationship with your boss. You want a good working relationship and you can't have a positive, rewarding relationship with someone who doesn't give a hoot about the organization.

In sum, find a good boss and establish a good working relationship. Keep them happy. Help them look good to their own bosses and meet their objectives. The rest is gravy.

© ASHLEIGH BRILLIANT 1981.   POT- SHOTS NO. 2180.

WILL ROGERS NEVER MET MY BOSS.

Ashleigh Brilliant

Reciprocal Interactions

> **All human interaction is reciprocal.** *It's probably the one most important principle we'll be talking about. Properly understood, it can be the single rule that guides you securely throughout your career.*
>
> —from *Working and Liking It*

We touched upon the concept of "reciprocal interactions" above in connection with your relationship with your supervisor. But this concept applies to all your relationships in an organization, including those with your superiors, your co-workers, and your subordinates. You can't expect anyone to consistantly meet your needs if you aren't consistently meeting theirs. This is an important point for managers and employees. It works both ways.

If you are a manager, your employees will not keep working for you if you don't work for them. If you are an employee, your boss will not work for you if you don't work for her. This is just the way life is. It is important to keep this in mind. Frequently someone will put forth ideas and suggestions (sometimes demands) that would clearly help meet their needs but which do not help others. A manager's idea that doesn't pay some dividends for employees is unlikely to be accepted and supported by those employees. An employee's idea that doesn't help management meet some organizational goal isn't likely to be adopted. There is no need to get upset over this reality. You just have to make your plans accordingly. If you have a good idea, you need to modify it so that it meets other people's needs as well. If the idea helps only you, why should anyone else buy it? The organization exists primarily to achieve some mission (make money, sell a product, provide a service). It doesn't exist just to make you happy. You can get rewards out of an organization, but only by giving it back something it wants in return.

This concept of "reciprocal interactions" is closely linked to "self-interest." Some employees get frustrated when their managers (or other employees) take actions which are detrimental to their interests or perceive ill intent on the part of management. People rarely do anything for the primary purpose of hurting you. They are simply pursuing their own interests. If you want to change their behavior or change policies, develop plans that help both of you. A plan that helps only you is not a plan. It is a fantasy. If it doesn't help both sides, it isn't viable. A realistic plan is one that benefits both sides. The best way to achieve your objectives is to help others achieve their objectives.

HOW COULD THE WAY I BEHAVE TOWARDS YOU

POT-SHOTS
NO. 1272.

POSSIBLY AFFECT THE WAY YOU BEHAVE TOWARDS ME?

Ashleigh
Brilliant

©BRILLIANT ENTERPRISES 1977

POT-SHOTS NO. 1667.

I WISH I KNEW MORE

ABOUT THE THINGS I'M NOT SUPPOSED TO KNOW ANYTHING ABOUT.

Ashleigh Brilliant

Effective Information Systems

As a rule, he who has the most information will have the greatest success.

—Disraeli

To succeed in an organization, you must know what is *really* going on. If you rely upon official communication channels, your information will be obsolete by the time you get it. If you act without knowing what is really going on, you may make major mistakes. If you don't have reliable information, get it before you act. The person with the most reliable information and best knowledge about trends will quickly advance over those people who have no idea about what is likely to happen tomorrow, much less next year.

In seeking information, don't discount that universally despised and universally utilized practice known as gossip. Gossip has a very negative connotation, but gossip is frequently the source of vital information. Gossip and the rumor mill can provide important leads, but you also need a way to confirm the information. This is where informal information sharing networks within organizations become so critical. The basics of information sharing involve the same principle we discussed above, reciprocal interaction. To get information from others, you must provide information to them.

You must learn who has reliable information and who does not. Stop wasting your time with the clowns and clods who have the great rumors which are always false and spend more time chatting with the people who seem to have a telepathic connection with the future. In the information age, you simply can't succeed without reliable information.

Persistence: If At First You Don't Succeed, Try, Try Again

> *The lack of perseverance is the reason most people fail in attaining their goals.*
>
> —Waitley/Witt, *The Joy of Working*

Persistence is a boring topic so I will only mention it briefly. However, just because it is boring to discuss, doesn't mean it is unimportant. In fact, many organizational analysts and career consultants consider persistence to be the ultimate key to success at both the organizational and personal levels.

Success seldom comes easily on the first try. What separates the successful from the unsuccessful is persistence. Successful people also fail occasionally but they do not let their failures defeat their spirit. Successful people learn from defeats, revise their strategy as needed and try again. And again. And again. Until they succeed. Unsuccessful people try something one or two times and when it fails they give up, usually passing the blame on to someone or something else, and learn nothing from their experience other than perfecting their scapegoating techniques.

Successful people expect periodic defeats, learn what went wrong and why, don't waste time looking for someone to blame, make necessary adjustments, and try again. If you are persistent, you will almost inevitably succeed. If you are not persistent, you will almost certainly fail.

Speaking of persistence, as you may note, I have included a "Pot-Shot" for each of the "10 Keys" except this one. I did look for one, but I didn't find it right off and I didn't have the persistence to keep looking. Sorry.

Be Nice to People

This is probably of greater importance than any other trait one may possess. Those with a good social personality get along well with others; they are always desirable associates.
—Ernest Holmes, *The Basic Ideas of Science of Mind*

Your relationships with people determine the extent to which you like your job and also the extent to which you are successful in achieving your objectives. Remember there is no such thing as "management." There are only people who happen to be managers. There is no such thing as "the work force." There are just people who happen to be workers. A key to achieving your objectives is to get along well with people, i.e. employees and managers. If you get a reputation as someone who is "difficult" to get along with, you are practically doomed. No one has time to deal with "difficult" people. So be nice to people. Don't hassle them. Smile. Is that so much to ask?

Part of getting along with others involves wasting time with them. I mention this because I am so bad at it. I like to plow into my work and get on with it. I'm uncomfortable standing around the water cooler shooting the breeze. Yet, these things are important. If you don't chit-chat with people, they will think you are rude. If you don't go to lunch with them, they will think you are stuck-up. If you don't go drink coffee (decaffeinated, please) with them, they will think you are obsessed with work. So accept the fact that you are going to have to use some of your time in maintaining friendly, cordial relationships—even if you would rather be in your office working on those dreadful reports and getting it over with.

IF YOU CAN'T GO WHERE PEOPLE ARE HAPPIER,

TRY TO MAKE PEOPLE HAPPIER WHERE YOU ARE.

Ashleigh Brilliant

©ASHLEIGH BRILLIANT 1983.

POT-SHOTS NO. 2975.

POT-SHOTS NO. 2055.

I BELIEVE, WITH GREAT SINCERITY,

IN WHATEVER IT WILL BENEFIT ME TO SAY I BELIEVE IN.

Ashleigh Brilliant

Loyalty: Be True to Your School

If people were always to speak their minds on issues both great and small, they would be considered insubordinate by the average supervisor and a threat to an organization by management.
—M. Scott Peck, *The Road Less Traveled*

Loyalty is not a favorite word of the New Agers. Many confuse being loyal with being "yes-men." New Agers tend to be loyal to ideas, causes, and their personal development but distrust the concept of loyalty when applied to their employing organization. Yet true loyalty is like true patriotism. It doesn't mean agreeing with everything your organization does, but rather trying to get your organization to live up to its potential and keep its ideals.

The key is to use appropriate ways of expressing your positions—not to abandon your positions. Criticizing your boss or organization in public will generally not win friends and influence people in the organization. If your company is about to dump hazardous chemicals in the city water supply and you can't convince them to dispose of the chemicals in a legal manner, then going to the press would be a commendable action. Of course, you will get fired and your company may shut down. But you have done the honorable thing. However, these situations are extremely rare.

Most disputes are not life threatening and going public with your differences between you and your organization is self-defeating. Everyone will see you as a trouble-maker and a crybaby. A good rule of thumb is never do anything to make your employer look bad to those outside of your organization. There may be exceptions but these should involve major disputes over major values for which you are prepared to leave the organization.

Most organizations have informal and formal channels for expressing concerns and raising objections to existing and proposed policies. Use those channels in a positive manner and you can fight for your position without fighting against your employer. Go outside those channels or use those channels in a negative manner using personal attacks and dissent will be seen as disloyalty. It is almost always a mistake to attack anyone within the organization personally. Depersonalize problems. Attack the problem, but don't attack people.

If your employer doesn't deserve your loyalty, go work for someone who does. Don't waste your life being a chronic complainer.

Be Responsible

True responsibility is an active caring and responsiveness to every-thing around us, a readiness to do whatever needs to be done.
—Tarthang Tulku, *Skillful Means*

Accept responsibility for your own life. Don't look for excuses and scapegoats. Nothing is more annoying than someone who is always trying to blame someone else for everything that happens to him. It is very easy to blame your manager for your failures. It is easy to blame the system. It is easy to blame co-workers. It is easy to pass the blame down to your employees.

Your life is your responsibility. You can't escape this reality. Trying to escape your responsibility will make you sound like a whining child.

Instead of inventing 50 ways to lose your way to work and arrive late, get to work on time. There is no excuse for repeated tardiness and trying to make excuses just makes you sound like a whimpering idiot. Take responsibility for your life and organize it so you can consistently get to work on time.

Instead of looking for reasons why you can't carry out your assignments, look for ways to do them. Every organization has people who have a strong and determined "no can do" attitude. Every time you ask them to do something, they give 96 reasons why it shouldn't be done rather than doing it. These people are almost universally despised and seldom achieve anything other than immortal status as Royal Pains in the Rump-a-Roni.

Have a Sense of Humor

The best ideas come as jokes. Make your thinking as funny as possible.

—David Ogilvy, Advertising Executive

Humor is the primary requirement to survive in a hostile environment. It is also a primary ingredient in preventing your work environment from becoming hostile. Humor is a matter of perspective. It involves seeing things in terms of their true importance. Humor is wisdom in action. It involves understanding that life is just a game and work is just a game within a game. And the purpose of games is not to determine winners but to have fun. Humor reflects the ability to see everything as a game. Show me a person with no sense of humor and I'll show you someone I don't want to work for and someone I don't want to work for me.

POT-SHOTS NO. 2745

I WANT TO BE TAKEN SERIOUSLY~

ISN'T THAT A JOKE!

© ASHLEIGH BRILLIANT 1983

Be Lucky

Every one of the unsuccessful people who answered said his or her life was influenced by forces beyond his or her control. Here lies the key to failure. When a person denies responsibility for the movement and direction of his life, he almost automatically fails.
—John T. Molloy, *Molloy's Live for Success*

Yes, I know. In a "New Age" book, there probably should not be any reference to luck. One theme among the New Age, New Thought, Positive Thinking, Science of Mind people is that there is no such thing as "luck" but that what appears to be luck is really the result of positive thinking and proper preparation. And I agree with that point of view to a large extent. We can create our own good fortune and we can certainly create our own bad luck. There is no doubt a person with a positive attitude is more likely to be lucky than a person with a negative attitude.

However, there are times when bad things seem to happen by pure chance—perhaps to test us, perhaps to no purpose. When a tornado hits your new branch office during its "Grand Opening" and destroys the building, your supplies, your inventory, and kills two of your best managers, it is difficult to attribute this wholly to negative thinking. Likewise, there are times when good things seem to happen by pure chance.

I have had several promotions, all deserved I might add, but two of them were the result of being very lucky. I will give just one example of how I got promoted thanks to a hurricane. In 1972, I was working in a small area office in upstate New York. In June of that year, Hurricane Agnes ripped into the East Coast. There was a massive amount of rain. Rivers flooded all over New York and Pennsylvania. Our office was totally destroyed and our files were washed away. Telephone lines were down for days. Through the luck of the lay of the land, my apartment house was undamaged and my roads were passable.

Since I had no electricity and was able to get my car out, I jumped in the car and drove away from the flood area to a nearby city which had another one of our branch offices. I reported to the new office. Of course, they didn't know what to do with me. And I didn't really go there to work or out of any sense of duty. I went there to find electricity (being a throughly modern person, I just can't imagine life B.E., before Edison) and out of curiosity to learn what was going on. The manager there called our regional headquarters in New York City and put me on

76

the phone to talk to our regional manager. They had no information from the flood zone and I was the first person they had heard from. I immediately became the contact person for all information going into and out of the flood sites for several days. I was able to talk with high officials who days earlier didn't know me from the man in the moon. Eventually, the rains stopped. We established a new operations center in the basement of a church and started trying to rebuild. The managers from regional offices came around almost weekly to check on our progress and they always stopped by to chat with me. Within a few months, I was promoted to a job in New York City. Now, it is true that I was an excellent employee at the time, but I could have done a great job in that little office for 30 years and no one would have known it. It was the hurricane and flood which set everything up for me.

There is a story within this story also. The local manager of my office was old, stupid, fat, ugly, and disliked everyone who didn't share at least three of those four characteristics with him. He especially disliked me and my just out of graduate school know-it-all attitude. Thus, while my immediate supervisor liked me and appreciated my good work, the office manager was not a big fan of mine and was likely to try to block any promotional options.

When the rains started in earnest, he left the office to go home and check on his house (a very nice house right on the river bank). He also left firm orders that none of the rest of us were to leave the office early under any conditions. We joked about waiting till the water was up to our necks before we could leave. His order was not as insensitive as I have made it sound (and I made it sound pretty insensitive when I reported it to our regional people) as his house was on a particularly dangerous site and our office was seemingly very safe behind the city's massive flood wall. Fortunately, quitting time arrived and we all left before the water came crashing over the flood walls and wiped our office off the face of the earth. As fate would have it, none of us in the office suffered any significant damage to our homes except the local manager whose home was severely damaged. (Yes, the angels were all on duty and performing well that day.) When news of his famous, I'm-abandoning-the-ship-but-you-have-to-stay-till-it-sinks speech got back to New York City, his recommendations pro or con on my career became irrelevant. He had his own problems, and he subsequently retired.

And so one little hurricane saved my career. What did I do to deserve this delightful twist of fate? Is it any wonder that my faith in

Lady Luck was revived? Do you wonder why I pay homage to the rain gods?

So while a positive attitude, good preparation, and a balanced approach to life generate many good breaks and help overcome many bad ones, it is still better to be lucky than unlucky. So My Friend (and anyone who buys my book has my eternal friendship, at least till my next book comes out), Good Luck To You Too.

POT-SHOTS NO. 1616.

THERE IS A DEFINITE REASON FOR MY SUCCESS:

THE REASON IS THAT I'VE ALWAYS BEEN VERY LUCKY.

©ASHLEIGH BRILLIANT 1979.

CHAPTER SIX

New Age Perspectives: Buzz Words, Cliches, and Various Nebulous Topics

Meetings

The more successful you become in your organization, the more time you spend in meetings.

—from *How to Make Meetings Work*

© ASHLEIGH BRILLIANT 1979.

POT-SHOTS NO. 1526.

An unfair method sometimes used to gain control of an organization is: to attend all the meetings.

Ashleigh Brilliant

One of the most dreaded words in almost every organization is "meeting." This word suggests a boring waste of time with little or no productive result. It has been estimated that as much as 70% of some organizations' time is spent in meetings. Yet few people receive any training in techniques for making meetings effective.

Successful meetings require a clear purpose, substantial advance planning, an appropriate structure, an appropriate setting, and an appropriate audience. Meetings are important. They cannot be totally eliminated—although they could and should be significantly reduced in most organizations. For an organization to be effective, it must find ways to conduct effective meetings.

Unions

The false distinction between labor and management is the seed of labor discontent and management inefficiency.
—Lawrence M. Miller, *American Spirit*

Although it may be difficult for some MBA'd yuppies to believe, there was a time during the industrial age that unions were a positive, progressive, humane force in our society. However, the value of the traditional union has declined with the decline of the industrial sector. Today, the traditional union is as outmoded as the traditional manager. There are still a few notable exceptions, but by and large, unions are now a counterproductive force and an ally of the dying age, not the New Age.

The New Age work environment requires direct and honest communication between managers and employees. Unions are an unnecessary filter for that communication. Many unions deliberately distort the communication for their own purposes. Even unions with good intentions are an unnecessary loop in the communication's process.

At a critical time when we must improve the efficiency of our organizations, many unions are still taking a short-sighted approach and continuing to defend obstructionist and incompetent employees.

The New Age is moving towards removing distinctions between management and workers. The trend is towards co-management and self-management. Unions are still trying to maintain distinctions, usually false and self-serving ones.

The fundamental problem with unions is that once established they develop interests separate, not just from management—which is expected, but from the employees as well. Many unions spend the vast majority of their time, money, and efforts fighting for institutional rights for the union (more time off work for union officials, travel benefits, priority parking, and other perks for union leaders, etc) rather than rights for employees. Unions become a third force draining resources from both management and employees.

In addition, in order to maintain the fiction that unions are still needed, some unions intentionally create conflicts and engage in pointless polemics against management to try to keep employees in an anti-management state of mind. In an era when management/employee cooperation is imperative for both groups, unions tend to be a very devisive force hurting management and employees alike with no one benefitting except a handful of union officials and a few incompetent employees who like to hide behind the union label.

This is not to condemn all unions and all union officials. There are still many good, well-meaning people in the union movement and many of them believe it is possible to create a New Age Union to correspond to the New Age Manager and New Age Employee. These progressive union leaders understand that cooperation must replace conflict to the maximum extent possible and that organizations must become more effective in order to survive.

What would a New Age Union be like? It would have the following characteristics.

1. A New Age Union would have a commitment to cooperation, not conflict. The union would try to create a sense of unity among employees and managers of an organization rather than dividing them into warring camps.
2. The New Age Union would take a balanced, holistic approach to the organization and not just make unrealistic, irresponsible demands that could threaten the success and survival of the entire organization.
3. The New Age Union would be democratic and equalitarian rather than representative and hierarchical. It would be a union *of* the workers, not just a union representing workers. There would be no distinction between workers and union officials because union officials would also work.

This last observation is a major point and major problem with many unions. The union leaders are not workers. They do not actually

81

work in the organization. They may have been workers at one time, but once they become full time union officials their interests are almost exclusively those of the union and only secondarily those of current workers.

Large national unions may need full time employees of their own. There is nothing wrong with a union having professional full time administrators, clericals, accountants, and attorneys to carry out duties for the union. But the union officials themselves, the people who set policy and make decisions, should be workers. This is the only way to have a true union of the workers, not merely a union allegedly for the workers. The most notable example of this type of New Age worker/ leader in the 1980's is actually from the Polish union Solidarity with its worker/leader Lech Walsea who put in his work day on the docks and ran the union largely on his own time and largely out of his own house.

Contrast this worker/leader union with many American unions run by high paid officials who haven't worked a day in the organization in decades, if ever, and who spend their time in luxury office suites thinking of ways of increasing their own power, income, and perks.

Are New Age Unions likely to develop in significant numbers in the United States? This is difficult to say. But it is clear that the old traditional unions are largely useless and they must either transform themselves into New Age Unions, give way to New Age Unions, or cease to exist. If unions continue in their traditional manner, they will destroy themselves and their organizations. Where you find traditional management and traditional unions in the same organization, you have a recipe for disaster. This was a major cause of the decline of the U.S. auto and steel industries. Neither management or the unions would take a holistic approach and put the interests of the entire organization and all the managers/employees ahead of the narrow interests of special groups.

Management must change and will change. The ascendancy of New Age Management is inevitable. The old ways just won't work today. It is less clear if unions will change. Many old time unions are so set in their ways, so full of hatred and distrust, so determined to create conflict, so determined to beat management, so obsessed with past wrongs (real or imagined), that their leaders would actually rather drag the company down into bankruptcy and see all the employees laid off than cooperate with management and pursue realistic objectives. Plus, many union leaders would die before they agreed to go back out and work in the organization.

Fifty years from now, almost all of these traditional unions will be gone. Some will have changed into New Age Unions and some will have simply gone out of existence. But as employees become more and more able and willing to represent their own interests and as New Age Managers begin to give employees greater responsibility and authority, employees will understand they don't need union bosses to represent them. The unnecessary division between management and labor will either be eliminated or modified so as not to be an impediment to cooperation and effective communication.

Every day we see more and more people in both management and the unions recognizing the need to alter the traditional and adversarial management-labor relationship. In October of 1987, the U.S. Department of Labor sponsored a most interesting four day conference in Los Angeles called "Beyond Adversity: Growth, Survival & Collective Bargaining." The timely theme of this conference was exploring "new ways of cooperation" as we head to the 21st Century. Management and union officials from around the nation and the world attended the conference. The conference included workshops on "Profit Sharing," "A Compact Instead of a Contract: The Wave of the 2,000's," "Work Worth Doing," "Alternatives to Arbitration," "Work Team Coordinators," and "Reshaping the Work Force and Work Place."

For managers, the best way to expedite the decline of the traditional, adversarial union is simply to practice the New Age Management philosophy. Where management continues to act like a bully and tries to kick the workers around, workers will obviously feel compelled to create their own bully to kick back. However, when management demonstrates (by its actions, not just its words) that it is willing to treat employees fairly, justly, holistically, and as responsible adults capable of self-management, then employees will respond by repudiating union officials who persist in acting irresponsibly.

POT-SHOTS NO.933

IF WE MAKE ANY MORE CONCESSIONS,

WE MAY LOSE SOME OF OUR ENEMIES.

Ashleigh Brilliant

©BRILLIANT ENTERPRISES 1976

California Time Warp

If America is open to innovation, innovation is California's middle name.
—Marilyn Ferguson, *The Aquarian Conspiracy*

Depending upon where you live, you may think the New Age is just a California phenomena. California has been called the international headquarters of the New Age. Marilyn Ferguson called it a "laboratory for transformation." There is no doubt that the New Age is most prevalent in the Golden State. However, whatever happens in California eventually, slowly but surely, spreads across the country and the world. In space, on the earth's axis, the United States turns east to west, and the rest of the country sees the sunshine hours before California. But in time, (not clock time), the world seems to spin the other direction. The West coast and especially California is always on the cutting edge of the future. The New Age dawned first in California. But in time, and in some places this means decades, the New Age will move across the entire nation.

For those who don't like change, like those people in the commercials who didn't like the drink "California Coolers," the New Age will be just another reason to hate California. But the traditionalists will have no more success stopping the flow of progress in time beyond California than they would have trying to change the way the earth rotates in space.

To those of you who fear that the winds of change may never reach you, (and studies have found the areas of the country most resistant to change to be Alabama, Mississippi, and Utah) remember you don't have to actually convince the ancient mariners of the old age to agree with you, just outlive them. Sooner or later, through retirement, death, or bankruptcy, they will be removed from the path of progress.

What is most frustrating is to live in one of the progressive centers (and California is only the first and most notable; Oregon, Washington State, Connecticut, Boston, Colorado, and pockets of New York and Atlanta are other areas on the edge of the future), and find that your particular organization is not adapting to the changing times. Yet this is a situation faced by many employees. Large institutions and public institutions are very slow to change in any area of the country. Small and medium-sized organizations must use progressive management techniques or they will go under quickly. But large corporations have so many assets that they can afford to be poorly managed and lose money

84

for several years before they are forced to face reality and change. Public organizations, including state, local, and federal governments as well as schools, are even morre difficult to change because they don't have a bottom line to measure their poor performance. Their managers and administrators are frequently covered by personnel regulations codified in state and federal law which make it virtually impossible to make meaningful change without legislative or Congressional action.

Therefore, if you are looking for a job with a new employer, be wary of large corporations and public employers. They are less likely to utilize progressive management techniques than many of the newer, smaller organizations.

A Parable: An 85 year old woman died and went to heaven. She had lived in California the last 60 years of her life. When she arrived in heaven, she was given the Grand Introductory Tour. After the tour, the angel asked her, "Well, how do you like it?" The woman replied, "Oh, it's nice, but it's not California."

For those of you who don't live in California, just remember, it's not just a state—it's a state of mind. There are little pockets of California all over the world.

© ASHLEIGH BRILLIANT 1982.

POT- SHOTS NO. 2619.

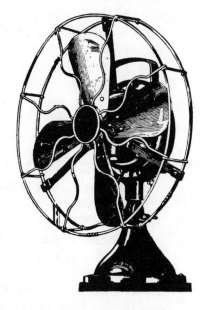

THE GREAT
WINDS
OF CHANGE
HAVEN'T YET
REACHED ME,

BUT
OCCASIONALLY
I FEEL
A SLIGHT
BREEZE.

Ashleigh Brilliant

The Unlearning Lab

The process for creating new ideas and the process for turning ideas into reality are entirely different. Most people and most organizations are much stronger in one area than the other. Organizations must find a way to integrate the two processes.
—Jay Davis, Management Consultant

One reason learning is so difficult is that it requires us to change our old ways of looking at things. Effective learning requires a significant amount of unlearning (that is, abandoning or modifying old ways of thinking).

As long as we can pile new facts on our old assumptions, things go rather smoothly. However, when the facts don't fit our assumptions, a major unlearning task is at hand. Many people will resist this unlearning until it is made painfully clear to them through various failures, defeats, and embarrassments that their old working assumptions must be changed.

The failure to examine basic assumptions is a fundamental problem in many organizations. For example, a manager decides to use participatory techniques and invites input from subordinates on a key decision. The employees provide good input, but then the manager does just the opposite of what everyone recommended. In this all too common situation, the manager has good intentions and tries to listen to the employee input. But the manager fails to really hear and understand the input because the ideas expressed conflict with some of the manager's basic assumptions. This makes "participatory management" appear to be a joke to the employees whose ideas are sought and then ignored.

It is important to periodically re-examine our basic assumptions. When we do, we frequently find that they no longer make any sense. They may have been valid at one point, but they have not been updated to stay in tune with the changing times. There is the classic story of the woman who whenever she cooked a roast trimmed an inch off all the way around, even though the meat appeared perfect. One day, her eight year old daughter, asked her why she always cut so much of the meat off. She replied that was just the way you made a roast. The daughter persisted as children are wont to do. Realizing she had no good answer, she called her own mother from whom she had learned this practice. The Grandmother thought and said that is just the way you do it because she had been taught that way by her mother. At the grandchild's insistence, the grandmother called her mother. The bottom line was that the great-grandmother had always trimmed the roast because all she had had at the time was a very small pan. She had always saved the excess meat to be cooked at a later time merely because it didn't fit her pan. This practice (which at one point made sense) had been passed on for generations (and become wasteful and unnecessary) based on assumptions that no one had challenged.

Many such assumptions and traditions have been passed along from generation to generation in this manner. At one point in time, they made sense. Today, they no longer fit the times.

Along with the "Question Authority" bumper stickers and the "Question People Who Question Authority" bumper stickers, we should also have some that say "Question Assumptions."

Simplify

Many people have a tendency, both at work and at home, of trying to do too many different things. This results in stress and ineffectiveness. To be effective, you must focus your energy into areas that really matter. Periodically, review your personal and work activities and eliminate those that don't really need to be done or which are not producing meaningful results in terms of your current objectives.

Let me give you a very simple example. As a child, I was a sports fanatic. At age 10, I could quote the batting averages of virtually everyone in a major league baseball uniform. Long into adulthood, I continued to study the sports page and keep track of almost every player on every team. Then, during a re-examine-my-assumptions-and-current-objectives session, I realized that this was largely a waste of time and that memorizing the sports page was not producing any meaningful results in my adult life. Since I do enjoy sports, I still check the scores daily and read the sports page once a week or so, but I spend only about 5% of the time previously spent. Likewise, in terms of watching games on TV, now I just watch the key parts of key games, such as the last quarter of a basketball game rather than the whole game.

At work, one of the great villains for most of us is reports. On one occasion, we had one of our secretaries quit and couldn't hire a replacement. This forced us to review the reports she had been preparing for computer input. We soon realized that 80% of what she had been working on was unnecessary.

Many useless reports are "required" by regional or national offices. A good approach to this problem is to stop sending clearly unnecessary reports for a while and see if anyone complains. You will likely find that years will go by and no one will ever notice you have stopped sending them because no one was looking at them anyway.

Ask yourself this question about all your activities, "Is this activity advancing my current objectives or is it just a useless habit left over from another time?"

Negotiations

The answer to the question of whether to use soft positional bargaining or hard is "neither." Change the game.
—Fisher/Ury, *Getting to Yes*

Negotiation is a fact of organizational life—many would add an "unpleasant" fact. A labor relations negotiator I once knew had a sign on his wall which said, "When you go to a hearing, one side wins, one side loses. But when you go to a negotiation, both sides lose." Unfortunately, all too often this is just the case. Many people think of negotiations as the process whereby each side gives up something it wants so everyone is equally unhappy with the result.

However, this need not be the result, and to have an effective organization it must not be allowed to occur with significant frequency. For in every organization there are hundreds of negotiations every day, some big, some small, some involving labor-management, some intra-management, some among employees. For an organization to maximize its effectiveness, these negotiations must produce positive results for all parties.

At a hearing, you have the classic win/lose situation. One side achieves its objective, the other side doesn't. At an ineffective negotiation, you get a lose/lose situation where neither side achieves its objectives. This is frequently called "compromise" and has given negotiations a bad name. At a win/win negotiation, both sides work together to create a solution that will allow each side to achieve its objectives.

I am not a naive pollyanna. In the real world, it is not always possible to create win/win situations, but most situations are amenable to a win/win resolution if the parties understand the fundamentals of effective win/win negotiations. The parties also need to understand that if too many win/lose or lose/lose situations develop, the effectiveness of the organization will be materially reduced. Every organization should teach win/win negotiating concepts to its employees and managers. The most basic concept simply involves the attitude with which the parties approach the negotiation. The parties should attack the problem, not each other.

POT-SHOTS NO. 1510.

IF YOU CAN'T GO AROUND IT,
OVER IT,
OR THROUGH IT,

YOU HAD BETTER
NEGOTIATE WITH IT.

© ASHLEIGH BRILLIANT 1979

Clothes

If you dress like a man of substance and integrity, you will, more often than not, be treated as such.
— John Molloy, *Dress for Success*

According to the old sexist cliche, "Men dress for success and women undress for success." To what extent this is true today in your organization, I will leave to your own idle speculation. However, many studies have shown (for both men and women) a positive correlation between appropriate attire and career advancement. The problem is that what is appropriate in one business or part of the country is not appropriate elsewhere.

Nevertheless, certain factors have emerged from the various studies in this area and it doesn't hurt to be aware of this information. Generally speaking, dressing "right" will not guarantee your success, but dressing "wrong" may well guarantee your failure. Use common sense. The basic rule of thumb is to study your own organization and determine what is the typical style of the successful men/women and then dress slightly more conservative than they do.

Remember clothes help project an image. Be sure the image you project is the one you want and the one that will help you attain your objectives. If your objective is to become President of the company, then you will dress differently than if your objective is to marry the President of the company.

People will react to you differently depending upon your style of dress. This is true at work and off work. I am treated far nicer in the financial district of San Francisco (by bank clerks, waiters, policemen, etc.) when I am wearing my three piece European designer suits than when I am wearing jeans. On the other hand, I am treated much nicer in the book and record shops in Berkeley when I wear my jeans and "Boycott South Africa" T-shirt.

Determine your objectives and make sure your clothes fit the image that will help achieve those objectives.

Statistics

> *Most statistics aren't worth the paper they are written on.*
> —Jay Davis, Management Consultant

It has been said that 65% of all statistics are of no value what-soever; that 30% are outright misleading; that only 5% are both valid and valuable; and that this statement itself probably falls within the first category. Yet, as anyone who works in the modern organization knows, we are all neck deep in statistics and they will not go away. What to do?

It is tempting to ignore all statistical data since so much of it is useless. However, without valid data and measurements regarding the work process, it becomes very difficult, if not impossible, to make effective decisions. Therefore, a good manager must do two things: work to eliminate the waste involved in accumulating and analyzing invalid data, and create systems to generate valid, understandable data that can be used effectively in the decision making process.

Data must meet three criteria. It must be valid, understandable, and helpful. If the data fails on any one of these three criteria, it is a waste of time to collect it. If the data isn't valid, it's worse than useless—it's misleading. If the data isn't understandable, it's worth-less—no matter how valid and potentially helpful it could be. If the data isn't helpful, it is again useless—even though it may be valid and easy to understand. These three criteria must be applied systematically to weed out the bulk of statistics so that there is time to focus upon the meaningful information that can be obtained.

Lawyers: Darth Vaders of the New Age

> *America has become overpopulated with lawyers. . . . the legal profession has transformed the American system into a govern-ment of the lawyers, by the lawyers and for the lawyers. . . . This has led to an explosion of litigation, which has burdened the paying public with billions in legal bills. These are paid by all the people in the form of higher costs, higher prices and lower produc-tivity.*
>
> —Jack Anderson

91

As a group, lawyers are one of the most reactionary forces in American society. In an age when we need cooperation and self-responsibility, they promote conflict and blame. Where we need unity, they promote division. Where we need honest communications, they practice the art of distortion in an effort to win legal games.

A recent study reported in the San Francisco Chronicle found lawyers bad for the economy. They are obviously bad for the total society. They have been called America's own home grown terrorists due to their explosive, random, and negative impact on the nation. It has been suggested that nothing would benefit our society more than a five year moratorium on all civil litigation and locking down the law schools until the next century. Of course, this will never happen. Lawyers are powerful figures in the Receding Age and they will not readily surrender their privileged positions.

Given the negative impact of lawyers on society in general, it is not surprising that they have had a very negative impact upon the employee-employer relationship as well. The number of so-called "wrongful discharge" cases has increased dramatically as lawyers have found a new area to exploit. Some employees now spend more time documenting their case against their employer for future litigation than they do performing their duties.

The fear of litigation impacts virtually every management decision. Many companies now refuse to provide references (good or bad) on current or former employees for fear they will be sued, and many employers are continuing to carry clearly incompetent employees that they would love to let go because the expense of litigating a termination is too high to risk. Large organizations have their own legal staffs to analyze various decisions with an eye towards minimizing litigation. This injects a high degree of timidity into the process as the staff attorneys see potential law suits everywhere and constantly advise against any type of bold action. Unless some controls are placed on lawyers they will eventually paralyze our society and turn us into a third-rate nation incapable of any decisive action.

Fortunately, there have always been a few dedicated attorneys who resist the power trips and who have worked for a progressive society. Today, in the San Francisco Bay Area and elsewhere, you can find ads for "New Age Attorneys" dedicated to resolving conflicts rather than promoting them. There is even a new law school in San Francisco designed to produce a new breed of public service attorneys.

Thus, if we can find a few rays of light in this darkest and most dreary of professions, then the light of the New Age is capable of reaching anywhere, perhaps even Mississippi or Iran. As for the rest of the legal profession, avoid them like they were the plague—for they do carry the plague of the Obsolete Age.

In the column quoted above, Jack Anderson writing with Dale Van Atta noted that a man named James K. Coyne has formed a group to try "to win the country away from the lawyers and give it back to the people." If you are interested in helping this worthwhile cause, contact the American Tort Reform Association, Seventh Floor, 1250 Connecticut Ave. N.W., Washington, D.C., 20036.

POT-SHOTS NO. 795

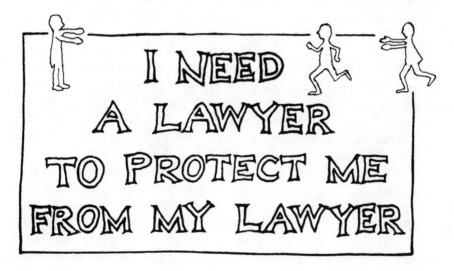

I NEED A LAWYER TO PROTECT ME FROM MY LAWYER

Ashleigh Brilliant

Stress: All Stressed Up and Nowhere to Go

Stress can be fantastic. Or it can be fatal. It's all up to you.
—Dr. Peter G. Hanson, *The Joy of Stress*

Constant change in the work environment creates opportunities, dangers, and stress. If there was little or no stress in our jobs, they would be boring and Boredom is surely one of the Seven Deadly Sins of the New Age. However, when there is too much stress, one can overload and become ineffective. Unfortunately, it is not always possible to control the pace of change or the pressure that can lead to stress.

If we have too little stress, we can initiate new projects to generate some activity and increase our stress to an optimal level. When there is too much stress, we can attempt to reduce it, but this is much more difficult. The best strategy for controlling stress is to learn to control our reaction to stress inducing events. In a real sense, most stress is self-created. While we cannot always control external events generating potentially stressful input, we can learn to control our reactions.

For example, if you are in a sales position or a public contact job, you will encounter a certain number of unpleasant people. There is nothing you can do to change this. It is the law of probability. A certain number of your public contacts will result in people being rude to you through no fault of your own. However, once you understand this and understand it isn't personal, you can learn to control your reaction to the rudeness. If someone wants to act like a jerk, you can't stop them, but let it remain their problem, don't make it yours.

When you accept responsibility for your own life, including your attitude and your level of stress, you learn that even when you can't change the situation, you can change your reaction to the situation. (Refer to earlier quotations from Ken Keyes.)

"Burnout" is an over-used and over-abused term frequently noted in connection with discussions on stress. Everyone who dislikes their job claims to have burnout. Some employees get burnout the first day on the job. Despite the abuse of the term by the free-loaders and goof-offs, there are real examples of burnout. In a nutshell, burnout exists when the rewards from doing something no longer seem sufficient to justify the effort to do it. It is easy to burnout on boring, repetitive tasks. It requires a real effort not to burnout in this situation. It also occurs when there is no opportunity for creativity and growth in a job. Few employees burnout while they are still growing and developing.

They do it when opportunities for growth have been exhausted. The best defense against burnout is the application of the New Age management techniques.

Money and Materialism

The rich man is the man who is satisfied with what he has.
—The Talmud

As Madonna put it in her own lovely way, we are living in a material world. It's nice to have money. Making money can be fun. Spending money is definitely fun. It's important for one's self-respect and self-esteem to be able to make a reasonable amount of money. One need not feel guilty about making or spending money. This is part of life. It is only when money becomes an obsession that throws the rest of one's life out of balance that money becomes a problem.

An interesting woman once explained this concept to me as follows. She said, "I would never date a man whose self-respect was so low that he had to have a $60,000 car." This point was well-taken. Generally, extravagance is a symbol of a life out-of-balance and a person with low self-esteem desperately seeking a crutch to prop it up. Of course, this same woman went on say, "I would never date a guy who drove an old clunker either. If he were that unsuccessful, he would probably have a major inferiority complex lurking just below his smug anti-materialist exterior." (It should go without saying that this woman lived in Los Angeles where the car is considered the ultimate expression of one's personality.)

A reasonable level of materialism is a reflection of a life-in-balance (a holistic approach) accepting material pleasures without becoming obsessed with them or using them in lieu of direct satisfaction of other needs. Putting too much emphasis on materialism (or anti-materialism) is an indication of a life out-of-balance.

To what extent is money an effective motivator for high performance on the job? This has been debated for decades. The best explanation is within the context of Herzberg's theory of motivators and demotivators. According to this theory, the presence of certain things will not motivate high performance, but the absence of them will serve as a demotivator and lower performance. Imagine you are working in St. Louis in August. The fact that your office has air conditioning will not, in and of itself, motivate you to peak performance. However, if the air conditioning system breaks down and takes two weeks to be repaired, the absence of air conditioning will likely serve as a demotivator and cause your performance to suffer. Likewise, the lack of adequate pay can contribute to poor performance, but a good salary cannot sustain high performance. To get high performance, the other needs/motivators must be brought into play.

For an employee whose life is balanced, this is especially true. There are specific limits to what such an employee will do for money. The type of employee who might be highly motivated by money is likely to be the one who desperately needs it to compensate for other imbalances. This type of employee is unlikely to be a high performer for long.

POT-SHOTS NO. 1024.

I HAVE POSITIVE PROOF THAT MATERIALISM IS EVIL

AND WILL REVEAL IT TO THE HIGHEST BIDDER.

Ashleigh Brilliant

© BRILLIANT ENTERPRISES 1977.

Careerists and Workaholics

*As the individual is drawn into the meritocracy, his working life is
split from his home life, and both suffer from a lack of wholeness.
Eventually, people virutally become their professions. . . .*
—Charles Reich, *The Greening of America*

Are there any meaningful distinctions between careerists and
workaholics? Possibly not, but let's see if we can't create some artificial
distinctions anyway. Careerists are people whose self-image is determined almost exclusively by their jobs. Virtually everything they do is
designed to advance their careers. They are defined by their jobs. When
you meet a careerist at a party, he immediately tells you his occupation.
Take away a careerist's job and he doesn't know who he is. He loses his
identity. His life is seriously out-of-balance. This particular disease is
called careerism.

Workaholics may or may not be careerists. Workaholics also spend
most of their time and energy on their jobs, but there may be different
reasons for their work pattern. They may not even identify with their
jobs. Work may simply be an escape, an effort to avoid dealing with life.
On the other hand, a workaholic may love his job and simply become
addicted to the pleasures of doing it and doing it well. It may just be too
much of a good thing.

Careerists may not even like their jobs. In fact, they may not even
work that hard. They may spend most of their time on organizational
politics and other schemes for advancement. Careerists are not so
much into work as into seeking identity through their jobs, their career
advancement, and the symbols of success.

A workaholic may be working to help others or to support a noble
cause. New Agers would be too wise to become careerists, but are
susceptible to becoming workaholics. If we are working on projects we
see as important to social transormation, it is easy to become obsessed
with the project and let other areas of our lives slide. We must all strive
to avoid this pitfall.

Managers must be alert to both careerists and workaholics, recognize the differences, and seek to help both move in the direction of
wholeness. Careerists are generally annoying people. They are easy to
spot and there is no reason to delay in providing them with proper
direction. Workaholics, on the other hand, may be giving you exactly
what you want in the short run—high productivity and a dedication to
duty. It may be tempting to let these situations drift for awhile and reap

the benefits of all this work. However, in the long run, the workaholic will burn out and the organization will suffer. The individual will certainly suffer. Living out-of-balance always takes its toll. The humane manager must try to assist as gently as possible in encouraging the workaholic to move towards a more balanced, holistic approach to life.

Organizational Politics

Excessive office politics weakens an organization and injures many innocent victims. . . . When people know what is expected of them, know how their results will be measured, and believe that what they are doing is important, the need for political maneuvering lessens.
—Andrew Dubrin, *Winning at Office Politics*

Like it or not, many decisions within an organization are based upon political (non-merit) considerations. Office politics (or more properly organizational politics since all types of groups are included) is a reality. Awards, promotions, job assignments, office windows, etc, are not always determined solely upon merit. All non-merit factors can be considered "political factors."

The lack of merit in the working world was one of the first big surprises to many of us Baby Boomers. Most of us spent our first twenty-plus years in the educational system. For most, this educational system was very fair and reflected merit to a large degree. If we were good students, we got good grades. The goof-offs got bad grades. This was fair. There was an occasional exception, such as the student of either sex who got good grades by sleeping with the professor. However, by and large, the educational system was fair. And even when the system wasn't fair, it didn't necessarily hurt you. If someone got a higher grade than they deserved, it probably didn't lower your grade.

When we got to the working world, the situation changed radically. Merit was often totally missing in the process. Thousands of factors went into decisions which didn't seem relevant. Especially in the areas of distributing awards, promotions, and other perks, merit was only one of many factors considered, and often a secondary factor at that.

Most Boomers now clearly understand that we all work in a political environment. However, this doesn't mean we are all office politicians. While we all probably make a few concessions to office politics (smiling and saying "good morning" to a supervisor when we feel like saying "blow it out your ear, bird brain"), there is a wide gap between the total political creature whose every move is designed to advance his career and impress the power brokers and the politically naive worker who just does his own thing and lets the chips fall where they may.

The New Age employee needs to be aware of office politics and the political climate within his organization. However, it is wise to avoid either extreme in behavior. If you think all decisions are based on merit and that you need not concern yourself with political factors, then you are very naive and you are going to be very disappointed with your career advancement. On the other hand, if you think politics is everything and spend all your time politicking rather than doing a good job, you will likely also be disappointed in your progress within the organization. Even if you should weasel your way to the top, you will have violated your own self-respect and lost the respect of your co-workers along the way. Office politicians are easy to spot and are seldom held in high regard.

The balanced approach is to recognize the factors in the political environment of your organization. Avoid making major political blunders that could destroy you. But don't rely solely or even primarily upon political factors to advance your objectives.

The New Age Manager should try to minimize political factors in the decision making process. No organization can expect to ignore merit factors and survive. Merit must become the primary factor in the reward system. If politics becomes the dominant factor, then employees will spend most of their time and effort attacking each other trying to gain the upper hand. Bad decisions will be allowed to go forward so that someone can get blamed for it later. Employees will start keeping book on each other. You will have to buy more file cabinets to hold all the "CYA" files. Don't let this happen. Keep political considerations to a minimum. Put merit first.

© BRILLIANT ENTERPRISES 1975.   POT-SHOTS NO. 801.

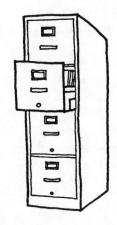

MY FILE ON YOU IS PROBABLY THICKER THAN YOUR FILE ON ME.

Ashleigh Brilliant

The Joy of Firing: And Other Less Humorous Disciplinary Actions

I estimate that it takes five years and costs a company $200,000 to fire one incompetent employee who persists in appealing the action in the courts. In the meantime, the company has probably hired 60 new incompetent employees. The $200,000 would have been better spent screening new employees and eliminating even half of the 60 new incompetents rather than in firing one old incompetent.

—A Federal Judge

Some may erroneously believe that the New Age Manager would never fire anyone but rather would find some way to motivate even the most uncooperative employee. Actually, termination is an important tool which most organizations should use more often.

Even with the best possible recruitment policies, a few people whose ability and interests do not coincide with those of the organization will slip through. If these people are intelligent and honorable, they will probably note the problem themselves and voluntarily leave to pursue something more to their liking. However, all too often, some of these misfits through ignorance, indifference, or laziness, will not move on voluntarily and will just hang on for months or even years unless the organization takes the initiative.

No effective organization can afford to carry any sizable number of incompetent, unmotivated, negative employees. Carrying goof-offs and militant obstructionists is an obvious recipe for disaster for the organization. In addition, it is not truly beneficial to the errant employees. Any employee who is not performing at a high level has clearly not found his "right livelihood" and is not getting the rewards from work that all human beings need. Thus, the organization is in reality taking a humane step (in all seriousness) to terminate such an employee and motivate him in a forceful manner to turn his career in a new direction.

This is not to suggest that termination is truly a fun action or that firing someone should be taken lightly. As mentioned before, the threat of litigation forces employers to take terminations very seriously. However, once an unacceptable situation has been identified and the employee has been advised and cautioned to correct the behavior/ performance, and if the employee is unable or unwilling to provide the organization with the type of work, attitude, and behavior the organization wants, the employee should be released. It does not benefit the employee or the organization to indefinitely prolong a situation in which neither is happy with the relationship.

Obviously, many preliminary steps may be taken to identify and resolve problems, and many employees who are seemingly incompetent and/or belligerent can be saved and turned around with skillful interventions on the part of managers. Managers need to make reasonable efforts to reform unsatisfactory employees. But there are limits to what managers should suffer. Managers cannot afford to spend so much time attempting to rehabilitate the misguided employee that they have no time for their good employees. If the employee does not respond to fair and reasonable assistance, termination is an appropriate tool.

While I heartily recommend terminations as an effective and necessary management tool, there are a couple of other disciplinary actions that I have found to be counterproductive and would not generally recommend. These are involuntary demotions and suspensions. Suspensions without pay are sometimes a prescribed part of "progressive discipline." Progressive discipline is a valid concept. It means you don't fire someone for the first minor infraction. A manager applies a series of progressively more severe acts following each infraction. The manager may begin with an oral counseling session, followed by some gentle reminders, followed by some not-so-gentle reminders, followed by a formal written warning, etc. Up to this point, I have no dispute with progressive discipline. However, some organizations then include suspensions from work in the process as a mandated step prior to termination.

Suspensions are generally self-defeating. It may hurt the employee to lose a few days of pay, but it also hurts the organization which presumably needs the employee at work. Why should the organization do this to itself? In addition, rather than motivating the employee to change his ways, more frequently this just makes the employee more bitter and less cooperative. If an employee doesn't respond to advice, guidance, counseling, cautions, oral warnings, and written warnings, then the employee is unlikely to respond in a positive manner to losing a few days of pay. Why prolong the conflict? Suspensions tend to be lose/lose situations.

Demotions are generally equally counterproductive when involuntary. If an employee is in the wrong job and everyone knows it and the employee voluntarily would like to try a different, lower-level job within the organization, then a voluntary demotion is certainly an acceptable alternative and is frequently in the mutual interests of the employee and

101

organization. I once asked for and received a voluntary demotion. I had been promoted into a very boring technical job which was clearly not my idea of a good time. There was an opening for an employee relations specialist in the personnel branch. Although it was at a lower level with slightly less pay, I jumped at the job. It turned out to be the best career move I could have made and my temporary step back was easily offset by several subsequent promotions. This type of voluntary demotion is a perfectly valid option and should be considered by employees and managers.

The type of demotion that is counter-productive is the involuntary demotion. If the employee doesn't want the lower level job and yet is forced to take it, this is another lose/lose situation. The organization may think it is being humane in not firing the employee and by giving the employee another chance. But this is not wise or humane.

If the employee doesn't want the lower level job and refuses to accept it without a fight, he is unlikely to make a maximum effort in the new job and his anger and hurt over the demotion will likely be directed at the employer in one form or another. The employee will probably be even less effective in the new job than in the old one. An outright termination is almost always preferable to an involuntary demotion for cause.

In sum, the New Age Manager need not be a wimp. While the New Age Manager wants to create a positive work environment and help employees to lead happy, productive lives, the New Age Manager should not hesitate to utilize appropriate disciplinary measures when employees are unable or unwilling to support the objectives of the organization. In taking decisive action to weed out the misplaced employees, the organization gains immediately and even the employee may gain in the long run by going on to something more compatible with his desires.

Discrimination

It's time we begin to realize that you and I are far more alike than we are different. We are all fellow beings travelling the road of life together.

—Ken Keyes Jr., The Hundredth Monkey

The problem of discrimination in the work place is extremely complex. There is no simple solution and no perfect solution. This is one of the most sensitive situations in the working world today. Even managers with the best of intentions and most pure of motives are likely to become involved in this controversy from time to time. The problem is multi-faceted. How can we recognize and address the more subtle forms of discrimination? How can we undo past wrongs without creating new wrongs? Does reverse discrimination generate a backlash which then perpetuates traditional forms of discrimination?

Factors such as age, sex, race, religion, and national origin are among the non-merit factors that do influence decision making. In some organizations, traditional forms of discrimination are still in existence, and in others, especially public organizations, reverse discrimination has become prevalent.

Can anything intelligent be said about this problem? No, probably not, but I'll try anyway. Most positions on issues related to discrimination are largely self-serving. Minorities argue with passion and sincerity about the dreadful conditions under which they have suffered and how this justifies preferential treatment today. Non-minorities present many elaborate and thoroughly rational arguments to the effect that they should not be discriminated against today and that the only way to stop discrimination is to remove race, sex, religion, etc, as factors in the decision making process rather than institutionalizing discrimination by giving minorities special treatment based upon non-merit factors. Both sides have good arguments and both positions are basically self-serving. Neither set of arguments does much to advance the cause of understanding.

In reality, all of us are discriminated against on a regular basis. It is a demonstrated fact of life that people, all types of people, tend to prefer other people that are as much like them as possible. Even in an office of all white males, the ones with certain backgrounds, perhaps Ivy League schools, will feel more comfortable and be able to talk more easily with others from the same background. This is not necessarily evil intent. It is just a truism that we all feel most comfortable and can communicate most easily with those whose background, attitude, and lifestyles are similar to our own. We feel most comfortable with people who look like us, talk like us, think like us, dress like us, act like us, etc.

Just think about it. When you walk down the street, go to a store to buy something, pass a co-worker in the hall, etc, you are more likely to get a positive response from someone similar to yourself. This doesn't mean other types of people dislike you. It simply means they don't understand you as well. They may fear you. They may feel uncomfortable. This unease causes them to treat you differently. This tendency to feel more at ease with people from backgrounds similar to our own is so ingrained in all of us that it would take a monumental effort to change it, if changing it is even possible.

So start by understanding that you will always be discriminated against, perhaps in subtle ways and perhaps in obvious and blatant ways, by almost everyone whose background is different than your own and that you too will likely discriminate against others simply because you feel somewhat less comfortable with them. Remember also that race or national origin or religion per se is not necessarily the issue. An educated, middle class white person will probably feel more comfortable with an educated, middle class black person than with an uneducated, lower class white person. Race, sex, national origin, and religion tend to be less important than educational background, income level, and social class.

Consider this example. If you are an educated, middle-class white person, would you prefer to live in an area comprised of educated blacks who work as doctors, professors, and accountants, or in an area comprised of uneducated whites with redneck tendencies who get drunk every weekend and ride through your yard on their motorcycles throwing beer bottles in your flower beds. The choice is obvious. My point is that income, education, and class (whatever that means) are more important than race, national origin, and religion in determining who you feel comfortable with.

The major kind of discrimination in the workplace over the past several years has probably been discrimination against young workers, specifically the baby boomers. The boomers were different. They had a whole new perspective. The older generation did not feel comfortable with them. They were not trusted. They were feared. And they were subjected to many kinds of subtle and blatant discrimination. (The Age Discrimination laws protect workers over 40 but not under 40.) Many organizations have built-in procedures to delay advancement. Perhaps one needs ten years of service to become a Vice-President or perhaps one can only be promoted once every two years. These are institutionalized methods of discriminating against young workers. Over the past several years, I have seen many situations wherein the older white, black, oriental, and hispanic workers felt more comfortable with each other than they did with the younger members of their own races. Again, the point is that people feel comfortable with other people who are similar to them. This is unlikely to change. We must all recognize our own tendencies.

Understanding the basis of discrimination and that all of us are likely to be discriminated against by anyone who is from a significantly different background, there are certain career conclusions that can be reached. If you are looking for a new job, you will likely be better off (in terms of fitting in, feeling good about the job, and career advancement) in an organization that consists primarily of other people very similar to yourself.

If you already work in an organization with a variety of employees, don't overreact to discrimination. Understand that it is not necessarily evil in intent and that creating personal confrontations over this issue may have more negative results than positive. Remember also that discrimination may be favorable to you as well as unfavorable. Those who feel comfortable with you are likely to react more positively to you. You may as well use that to your advantage. If you have a choice between two division leaders, you will probably be better off working for the one that is the most like you in terms of age, race, class, and attitude.

If you are the victim of negative and blatant discrimination, of course you have recourse to various EEO appeals procedures and ultimately litigation. However, this is generally counterproductive, especially for institutionalized reverse discrimination. You seldom achieve your objectives by fighting with your employer. If the situation is totally intolerable, go elsewhere. It is easier and faster and better for your peace of mind. If you fight with your employer, you may be able to win the battle, but you will likely lose the war. If the conduct of your employer is especially egregious and should be stopped in the public interest to prevent future acts of illegal discrimination, then consider filing a formal EEO complaint *after* you have left. But there is seldom anything to be gained from continuing to work for an employer with whom you are fighting.

While from an employee's viewpoint, there may be advantages to working in an organization with other people very similar to the employee. If you are a manager, you need to understand the importance of having a variety of different people working for you. If you deal only with people just like yourself, you are impaired by virtue of a very limited perspective.

For example, if you only served or sold to people just like yourself, then you might not need a variety of viewpoints. If you sold only to Albinos between 45 and 55 years old, it might not hurt your organization if you only recruited and promoted Albinos between 45 and 55. However, very few organizations have a clientele so limited. Most organizations must sell to or service the entire range of people within the society. Therefore, it is important in terms of both fairness and efficiency to have all these groups represented within the organization so that their needs can be understood and various viewpoints expressed in the intra-organization decision making process.

Thus, it is in the interests of both social justice and effectiveness for organizations to recruit and promote people from all segments of society. In this regard, we must all guard against the tendency to feel more at ease with people very much like ourselves and not let this tendency blind us to the value of having other types of people working in key positions and providing input into major policy and personnel decisions.

One of the things we all need to do is to focus more upon the many aspects we all have in common rather than upon the few areas where we are different.

As was noted, this is a complex topic. People of good will disagree on many points related to discrimination. It is one of the most sensitive issues in the work place. In recognition of how sensitive this topic is, I have declined even to include a cartoon on this matter as I am sure whatever it was it would manage to offend someone.

Women: The Feminization of the Work Place

> As the numbers of women increase in the ranks of corporate managers, their presence will be characterized less by the abandonment of feminine qualities and more by the expansion and development of those qualities within the unified culture of the organization.
>
> —Lawrence M. Miller, *American Spirit*

We now turn to my very favorite topic—women. There has been a dramatic increase in the number of women in the work force over the past two decades. Regrettably, few of these women have yet reached top positions. Therefore, they have not had as much of an impact on management as might have been expected. In addition, of the small number of women who have made it into key positions of power, many of them have felt compelled to try to emulate their masculine peers and out-macho the men.

Likewise, most of the first wave of Baby Boomers, men and women, to achieve success within large organizations did so by adopting the traditional approach to gain quick acceptance. Even in politics, the first Boomer to seriously seek the Presidency was Albert Gore who until recently was best known among Boomers for his wife's misguided crusade to censor rock music—the very music that has played such a large role in the Boomers' lives. And, of course, the first Boomer to become a token on a national ticket was Vice-President J. Danforth Quayle, an opponent of women's rights and a man whose opposition to the war was limited to joining the national guard. So it is not unusual for the first wave of any group (be it women or a new generation) in any area (be it politics or business) to be unrepresentative of the larger group. These people got to be the first wave by playing by the existing rules rather than trying to change the rules. The next wave, the larger wave, will change the rules.

As the New Age unfolds, we can expect to see major changes in this area and expect to see management feminized to a significant extent. Organizations not only need women in the work force, organizations need the skills generally associated with women to be reflected in the management process. These skills are sometimes called "skills of the heart." When these skills, which both sexes are capable of utilizing, are incorporated into the management approach, then we can move away from the traditional macho approach of managing-by-kicking-around.

The progressive organization needs to bring women into key positions in significant numbers, encourage them to retain and use their feminine traits rather than emulating the traditional male models, and encourage the men within the organization to develop and utilize these so-called feminine skills (or some would say right-brain skills) as well. When this happens, we will see organizations move away from the traditional male oriented decision making processes (militaristic, authoritarian) and towards a more human oriented approach involving consensus, cooperation, and compassion.

Management by Cliche

The key to working effectively is to concentrate on what is really important to you (your primary priorities) and not get sidetracked by the virtually infinite number of secondary priorities and concerns.

—Jay Davis, Management Consultant

The following are a few cliches which have been used so much that they have lost their impact but which are important nonetheless.

The Golden Rule of Management

Many people looking for a quick and simple guide for managers have advocated the so-called Golden Rule of Management. This rule simply states that managers should treat their employees like they want to be treated by their own bosses. This is a fairly good guideline. Many times I have seen managers complain about the way their supervisors treat them and then go right out and do the same thing to their own employees. So keeping this simple rule in mind would be somewhat helpful.

However, many other management analysts have noted that the rule is too simple and doesn't go far enough. A given manager may adhere to the military model and not mind being ordered about by his own manager. If this manager takes the same approach to his own employees, those employees may not accept this approach so readily. Thus, some people modify the Golden Rule to say—Treat your employees in the same manner in which you would want to be treated if you were in their position with their values. This is not nearly as catchy, but is more helpful.

Put People First

Another short, simple phrase which would be helpful if followed. Many organizations get so caught up in their technology, sales campaigns, procedures, policies, etc that they lose sight of the most important part of any organization—its people.

Health is Wealth

Staying healthy helps make you a better worker/manager. Keeping your employees healthy makes your organization more effective. More and more companies are actively promoting "wellness" through exercise facilities, expanded health services, etc. These are positive trends. The progressive organization must explore all avenues for promoting good health. Some of these avenues may include minimizing travel schedules that are disruptive of an employee's personal life, providing adequate vacation time, offering periodic sabbaticals, offering on-site education on key issues such as nutrition, drug abuse, AIDS, disease avoidance, and banning smoking.

Smoking is an especially important topic at present. The medical information is overwhelming that smoking is bad for a person's health. Studies have shown that smokers are absent from work due to illness much more often than non-smokers and that health care costs for an organization are higher for smokers than non-smokers. Recent studies lend more and more credibility to the position that even non-smokers may be adversely affected by being in an area where people smoke. With all these studies and evidence at hand, the progressive organization must move towards severely restricting smoking.

In terms of good health from the individual's perspective, we all need to follow the basics which include adequate sleep and relaxation, a balanced diet, no smoking, minimal caffeine, minimal alcohol, no illegal drugs, minimal legal drugs, plenty of exercise, etc.

Again, as in virtually every area, it is important to keep everything in a proper perspective and proper balance. Unless you have a specific medical problem it is not necessary to eliminate all alcohol, all sugar, all caffeine from your diet or make extreme efforts to pursue some particular diet. Another area where people go to absurd extremes is exercise. It is not necessary to be a marathon runner to get adequate exercise. Running a few miles a few times a week should suffice. People who become obsessed with exercise and spend hours and hours every day running or pumping iron can generally do so only at the great expense of creating a serious imbalance elsewhere in their lives. Again and again, the keys are proper perspective and proper balance, taking care to see the whole picture and meet all your needs.

That Which is Rewarded Gets Done

This is another cliche which is so true that it gets overlooked. If an organization isn't getting quality work, then it is very likely that the organization isn't rewarding quality work. Management frequently gives lip service to some objective, but doesn't truly reward the behaviors necessary to achieve the objective. Then, management appears surprised and confused when the objective isn't achieved.

Organizations should study closely precisely when they do reward. What type of behavior/performance earns promotions, awards, perks, recognition, status, etc? If you reward cautiousness, you'll get cautiousness. If you reward risk-taking, you'll get risk-taking. If this rewarded behavior is not the behavior an organization really wants, stop rewarding it. Employees are not stupid. They can see what gets rewarded and what doesn't. They will know that if management says it wants "A" but rewards "B", they are going to do "B."

Make sure you reward what you really want because what you reward is what you'll get.

Two Brains are Better than One

Unlike finite industrial resources such as oil, ore, and iron, there is an inexhaustible supply of knowledge, concepts, and ideas as people gain further education.
—S. Normal Feingold

We have largely discussed the holistic approach from the stand point of meeting the full range of human needs. In considering the whole person, it is also necessary to consider the whole brain. Scientific research has indicated that each person has two separate brains—the so-called right-brain and left-brain. Although these brains are connected, they function very independently and produce significantly different perspectives from the same person.

The left-brain is involved with rational, logical, linear, analytical, verbal, sequential, and goal-oriented activities. The right-brain is involved with intuitive, artistic, emotional, playful, physical, and visual activities. Virtually everyone uses both sides of their brains but most people have a strong tendency towards one side or the other. Most organizations are heavily oriented towards the left-brain and need to use more of the right-brain perspective. It is important for individuals and organizations to be aware of these different perspectives and take necessary action to integrate both types of thinking to ensure that they are getting the whole picture. We can't operate with half-baked ideas—ideas that haven't been considered from both sides of the brain.

Culture: Or, This Organization Has No Class

Though change is inevitable, change for the better is a full-time job.
—Roger Smith, CEO, General Motors

110

A few years ago the word "culture" burst upon the scene to become a major buzz word in organizational analysis. At the time, a running joke was as follows. First Person: "What is the culture of your organization?" Second Person: "Our organization doesn't have any. In fact, this place doesn't have any class at all." This was then followed by numerous variations on the theme. "In fact, our boss thinks Picasso is a type of peanut." "In fact, our boss thinks that Brooks Brothers is a country music band."

Despite all the jokes about the term "culture," it is an important matter. Culture within this context is generally defined as the organization's methods for dealing with its people and their needs. Just as societies and nations have different cultures, organizations have different cultures. Having worked in organizations with strong, positive cultures and organizations with weak, negative cultures, I have observed the dramatic difference. A positive culture will not guarantee success, but a negative culture will ensure failure. Don't let the buzz-wordish nature of this concept blind you to its importance. To a large extent, this entire book has been dealing with ways of changing an organization's culture by changing the way the organization treats its employees and helps them meet their needs.

Performance Standards

> *Of all the organizations I have studied which had written perform-*
> *ance standards, less than 10% get enough benefit from the written*
> *standards to justify all the time and effort it takes to write them.*
> —Jay Davis, Management Consultant

Many organizations develop written performance standards so that employees know precisely what is expected of them. This is great in theory, but in practice many of these performance standards are worthless. Performance standards frequently fail for one of three reasons.

1. They are not specific. Some written standards are just verbose variations on "do a good job." This is not specific. The employee still doesn't understand exactly what she is supposed to do. A specific standard would be "Sell at least $100,000 worth of equipment each month."
2. They cannot be measured accurately. It doesn't help to have specific standards if there is no mechanism for accurately mea-

suring performance to determine if the standards are met. For example, if you require a typist to have 192,000 key strokes per day but you have no way to count the key strokes, then the specific standard is still worthless.

3. They are not realistic. Assume in the above example that the typist works on a computer system that can keep track of key strokes. Then, we have a specific standard (192,000 strokes per day) and we can get a daily print out showing how many key strokes were input. However, if the standard is unrealistic, the employee will become discouraged trying to meet it and supervisors will have to ignore the standards or fire all the typists. Someone typing 80 words a minute with an average of 5 key strokes per word would type 400 key strokes per minute. This would be 24,000 per hour and 192,000 per eight hour day. Is this realistic? Not where I work. Few typists could maintain that pace for eight hours. And trying to maintain that pace day after day would be virtually impossible for all but the absolute super stars.

Written performance standards are a worthy idea. However, they must be realistic, specific, and measurable. If they fail on any one of these three points, the standards are useless and may even be counterproductive.

Recruitment: The First Deadly Mistake

I have yet to find a sizable company of any type that couldn't be made more effective by replacing 10% or more of its current employees. There is always deadwood.
       —Jay Davis, Management Consultant

The effective organization begins with an effective recruitment system. An organization's most important resource is its people. An organization can be no better than its employees. These employees don't just materialize out of thin air. They must be recruited. A good recruitment system provides a source of top notch employees. A poor recruitment system brings in losers, boozers, and snoozers and dooms the organization.

Although the mistakes of the recruiter can be undone, it is extremely costly to do so. A bad employee can be terminated, but it may involve a minor war with subsequent litigation. And even if the organization is successful and can get rid of a poor employee through hook or crook, the organization will likely have wasted considerable resources trying to train him.

There is simply no substitute for hiring the right kinds of people initially. This is an absolute must. It is vital that those individuals involved in the recruitment process know exactly the type of employee the organization needs and how to find them and hire them.

One important tool in the effective recruitment process is the personality profile. It is not enough merely to match skills with duties. It is also important to match employee attitudes and personalities with organizational philosophy and the requirements of a particular job. An aggressive, independent attitude may be perfect in the research department, but not in the records maintenance section where willingness to passively follow uniform rules may be more important. A certain personality may be suited for the accounting branch, but not the sales department. There is no "right" personality per se, but the personality and attitudes should fit the particular job.

One type of personality profile is the Briggs-Meyer Analysis which categorizes individuals on four areas; aggression, people-orientation, patience, and commitment to quality. This can be a useful tool, but there are several varieties of personality and attitude tests available.

Some potential employees may object to taking tests, especially intelligence, attitude, and personality tests. But show me a person who refuses to take tests and I'll show you someone who probably has something to hide. Intelligent people are not afraid of intelligence tests. People comfortable with and confident of their personalities and attitudes are not afraid of personality tests. Losers in any area are always afraid of tests and understandably so. Winners welcome the opportunity to display their abilities and talents.

Once on the payroll, every day will be a test. If someone can't take the pressure before you start paying them, they probably also won't be able to take the pressure afterwards. If they have an excuse for why they don't perform well on tests, they will probably delight you with dozens of interesting excuses as to why they don't perform well on the job either. Never hire anyone without extensive testing. Credentials mean little or nothing. References mean little or nothing. Do your own objective testing and constantly validate your results to make sure you are testing for the right skills and traits.

Major efforts must be made upfront to get the right kinds of employees. An ounce of effort in the recruitment process is worth a pound of effort anywhere else. Don't short change recruitment. Good employees are the ultimate key to success. Hire winners and your organization will be a winner. Hire losers, and kiss it all goodbye.

Training

Learning is as strategically critical to a knowledge-based, post-industrial economy as steel was to a materials-based, industrial economy.
—Lewis J. Perelman

It's often been noted that in a budget crunch training is the first area to be cut. This is unfortunate but somewhat understandable. Many training sessions are a total waste. The trainers don't know what they want to accomplish, how to accomplish it, or how to measure to see if they have accomplished it. Training is frequently boring. No one learns when bored.

The effective organization must have an effective training branch. This will become more and more vital in the future. The skills and knowledge that a new employee brings in the door will not be enough, and even if they were enough, as things change new skills and knowledge will be needed. The effective organization will need an ongoing training process that continually provides managers and employees with new information. Our society made a major mistake in making the educational process a low pay, low status situation. Our society is now paying dearly for this misappropriation of national resources with our second rate school system. (My favorite illustration of this point is a friend of mine who was an excellent teacher but couldn't live on the salary. So he quit and took a much higher paying job selling dog food. As long as we pay dog food salesmen more than teachers, we can expect to have dogs that eat as well as children and children who read as well as dogs.)

Organizations must not compound this error by relegating the training branch to second class status. The training branch should be staffed with top people and provided with appropriate benefits to keep them employed and happy.

Once trainers are given this high status, high pay situation, they should be held strictly accountable for producing meaningful, measurable results. Almost every class should have before and after studies to determine whether or not the training produced the intended result. It does no good to give your managers a class in New Age techniques if they go back to the office and fall right back into the same old ruts. There should be a follow through. In fact, it is a mistake to think of training as just what happens in a classroom environment. The training may start in the classroom, but effective training requires continuing input via consultation, mentoring, and monitoring. Trainers should be more than classroom teachers. They should provide continuing input via analysis, advice, consultation, and mentoring. Trainers must be a combination teacher/consultant/analyst. Effective training is not just a one shot event but a continuing process.

POT-<u>SHOTS</u> NO. 1998

Entrepreneurs

I worked for three companies over a five year period. They all treated me like a machine with no human feelings. So I started my own company. And now I can treat my own employees like machines.

—An anonymus entrepreneur

One of my favorite songs from the glory days was by Steven Stills called "If you can't be with the one you love, love the one you're with." This has been perverted into "If you can't get the job you love, love the job you've got." And there is some validity in that approach as we have discussed earlier.

However, there is another option and that is to create your own job by creating your own organization. The baby boomers are the most entrepreneurial generation in history. They have made the entrepreneur a modern hero. One of the primary reasons for the high number of boomers quitting their jobs and starting their own companies is that the organizations they worked for are such terrible places to work. Many people have concluded that it is easier to create their own businesses than to change the organizations that they work for into an enlightened employer.

How many truly happy employees have you seen give up comfort and security and risk their life savings on a new business venture? The people who drop out and blaze a new trail are by and large people who were fed up with their jobs and felt compelled to make a change. The entrepreneurial option provides another exciting possibility for employees and presents another serious challenge for existing organizations. Employees now have more options than ever. If organization "ABC" takes an insensitive approach to its employees, the employees can go work for an employer who will treat them like human beings or the employees can create their own organizations. There is no way to force good people to stay with you. To keep good employees, management must keep them happy. Otherwise, good employees will leave and the organization will be left with nothing but the losers who lack the initiative and/or ability to find another job or start their own companies.

The Secretary: The Unsung (and Underpaid) Hero of the Modern Organization

A good secretary is worth her weight in gold.
　　　　　　　—Jay Davis, Management Consultant

If there is any job in an organization more important than that of secretary, it doesn't immediately spring to mind. The secretary transforms potentialities into realities. I have seen a good secretary make an incompetent boss appear to be right on top of things and I have seen an incompetent secretary make an excellent manager appear to be an idiot. In an information based work environment, there is no way to overestimate the value of an excellent secretary. A good secretary does not just type letters and answer the phone. A good secretary is really an administrative assistant and a key player on the management team.

The following story shows the importance of having a secretary who can do more than type. Once I had a secretary who was as attractive as any straight man could ever hope to find sitting outside his office door. One day I drafted a memo to my boss decrying the fact that all my confidential intra-management memos concerning strategies for hearings and negotiations with the union seemed to turn up in the union's hands before the ink was dry. After typing the draft, the secretary brought it to me and explained that she knew how the union got everything so quickly. How? She thought anything referring to the union was supposed to be sent to them so she had been sending the union president copies, proving once more that beauty is not everything.

Because the boss/secretary relationship is so critical, many individuals bring their secretaries with them as they advance from job to job up the organization. In fact, one acid test for whether or not a given manager has a truly significant role in an organization is to ask—does the manager have the authority to select his/her own secretary? If a manager must just accept any secretary that is assigned to the position, then this manager, more often than not, is just another flunky. Whereas if the manager has the authority to select/hire a secretary of her/his own choosing, then you are probably dealing with someone of substance in the organization. This rule of thumb is not 100% accurate, but it is close enough to be a reliable indicator.

117

Despite the vital role played by the secretary, many organizations still undervalue this function and pay secretaries rather poorly. For an organization to be effective, it must avoid this mistake. Underpaying your secretarial staff is a good way to undermine your organization. If your organization sets a limit on the amount of salary that can be paid a "secretary," then use a more appropriate job title, such as office manager, office coordinator, executive staff assistant, or administrative assistant. The point is to find a way to pay secretaries for their true value so that they are not forced to leave the job.

One unfortunate result of low salaries is that some excellent secretaries transfer into other fields (such as sales or a technical job) in order to earn more money and in so doing frequently find themselves in fields where their performance falls off dramatically. This can be avoided by paying secretaries the salaries they deserve.

This is, of course, one of the arguments advanced by many women's groups in support of the concept of "comparable worth." While this concept has some troubling aspects, it also raises some important issues. It is safe to say that if your organization pays your gardeners and janitors more than your secretaries, then your facility will probably still look clean and well maintained when your secretary performs her final duty and files your bankruptcy papers.

In summary, think of your secretary as an "assistant manager", and pay accordingly.

Working Parents

> *It is certainly possible to have it all—to have a successful, rewarding career and still be an effective, loving mother. All you need is good planning and organization—plus, of course, an understanding boss, a supportive husband, temperamentally easy children, four loving grandparents within a ten mile radius, a cleaning person, a gardener, a nanny, and 48 hours a day.*
> —Judy Pantusi, a wife, mother and Program Analyst

One of the major developments of our era is the two-career couple. While many of these couples have chosen to remain "child-free," most do have children. This has created many new and unique problems for employers and employees alike involving issues such as child care, sick care, vacation scheduling, etc. In addition, single parents and divorced parents with custody experience many of the same problems and often their problems are even more difficult to address.

118

Thus, as never before, employers who want an effective work force must help employees find ways to balance work responsibilities with family responsibilities. During the 1988 Presidential campaign, for the first time, all the major party candidates issued positions related to day care. Whenever politicians face up to a new problem, you know it must be a clear and present reality as politicians will avoid any controversial issue as long as it can possibly be ignored.

The problems related to day care are complex and not easy to resolve. A simple solution is for the employer to provide on-site day care services for employees and this may be an ideal solution in a few locations. However, in large metro areas with long commutes from many different directions (like New York and Chicago), most parents would not want to bring their children with them in the car, train, or bus. Thus, in a major city, employers wanting to provide day care may have to establish eight to ten different centers in various outlying communities. This is seldom feasible.

An alternative is to provide a credit of "x" amount of dollars for employees to obtain their own day care services, but this becomes a bonus paid to working parents that is resented by employees without children.

A more practical approach used by some innovative employers is to include day care benefits in a "smorgasbord" of benefits from which employees may choose a certain number of alternatives. This way a working parent may choose a day care credit and an employee without children could choose another benefit of equal value (perhaps stock options, added vacation time, or an enhanced retirement plan). A parent with older children may prefer a college tuition credit. Someone covered under a spouse's health plan may not need duplicate health coverage and trade health benefits for day care. This smorgasbord approach allows all employees at a given level equal benefits but allows them to choose the precise types of benefits they most desire based upon their individual needs at the moment.

Organizations that cannot afford to provide day care or a day care credit should at least provide an extensive referral system to help parents find good day care in their areas.

In addition, there are a number of other ways a good employer can assist working parents. The employer can provide information and training on effective parenting techniques, time management, and other matters of special relevance to parents. But probably the most important thing an employer can do is to provide a flexible leave policy. With last minute emergencies and unexpected illnesses, working parents are not likely to have an attendance record as admirable as a non-parent. Employers need flexible hours and assignments to address this reality. Otherwise, an employee is put in the impossible position of being forced to choose between family obligations and work responsibilities. With flexibility and reasonable advance planning by both employer and employee, this type of predicament should be eliminated or at a minimum drastically reduced.

The working parent is the new reality. Employers may not like it, but it is a fact that must be faced. The effective organization must find ways to assist working parents. We have only begun to scratch the surface in dealing with this problem.

Computer Babies

> *The flurry created by the Computer Babies' move into the work force continues. Personal freedom and self-expression on the job are a central issue of the new workers, approached in their own unique way. The image of the Computer Baby work force is that of young workers wearing sunglasses and having their ears plugged in to their own private music.*
> —R. Eden Deutsch, Human Relations Consultant

A new generation is now beginning to enter the workforce in significant numbers. So far no generally accepted term has emerged to classify this second post-war generation (the way the term Baby Boomer did for the first post-war generation). However, of the many terms being used (like "Baby Busters") my favorite is "Computer Babies." I don't know who coined this phrase but you see it in magazines everywhere. The concept refers to the fact that this generation currently entering the workforce is the first generation to go to work *already* possessing advanced computer skills. Boomers may have popularized the computer, but most had to learn computer skills as adults. The Computer Babies have been raised on computers, trained to use computers in school and at summer camps, prepared their home work on home computers, typed their book reports and term papers on word processors, and entered the job market with advanced computer skills as of their first day at work.

The Computer Babies share the Baby Boomers scorn for traditional management practices and the Computer Babies are even less tolerant of illogical, ineffective processes. Having been raised on the ultimate logical/rational tool (the computer), the Computer Babies have zero patience for illogical management practices and organizations that do not utilize the very latest high-tech systems. Since the Computer Babies are part of the baby bust and since this demographic fact will create high demand for the limited supply of new workers, organizations are going to have to expedite their shift to New Age management practices and stay on the cutting edge of new technology in order to be able to attract and retain top employees from the Computer Baby generation.

Some traditionalists had hoped that the Computer Babies would be a more traditional generation and reverse some of the trends started by the Boomers. This hope was based largely upon some polls and studies which showed Computer Babies were not as "liberal" politically as the Boomers had been. However, the traditionalists' hope has not materialized. The Computer Babies approach to the work place is following the Boomer's trends and not reverting to the old traditionalist approach.

How do we account for the fact that the Computer Babies appear to be simultaneously less liberal politically and yet anti-traditional in terms of work/management practices (as well as in other lifestyle areas)? To some people these attitudes appear to conflict, but I am not so sure. Computer Babies may have rejected traditional liberal politics for the same reason they rejected traditional management practices. Both were ineffective. I have seen no studies to show that Computer Babies are opposed to social justice, equal opportunity, peace, protecting the environment, etc. However, they do appear to be disillusioned (as are many others in all age groups) with traditional liberal, New Deal, big government approaches to achieving these goals. Given the intolerable levels of inefficiency in the large public bureaucracies, it is hardly surprising that even people who support the overall objectives of these programs have serious reservations about continuing to pour more money into these ineffective systems. (And, of course, one of the many reasons why these public bureaucracies are so inefficient is that most are locked firmly in the grasp of traditional management practices.)

However, let me quickly end this section before I digress too far into the quicksand of politics. My point is that regardless of their political inclinations the Computer Babies are not sympathetic to the traditional management practices and any hopes that the traditionalists had that the Computer Babies would try to roll back the clock on the emerging holistic management trends are simply unfounded. The Computer Babies will demand these trends be expedited, not reversed. Traditional management practices will work no better (and in fact worse) on the Computer Babies than on the Baby Boomers.

Self-Esteem and Self-Image

Man's best friend is his self-image.
—Dr. Maxwell Maltz, *Psycho-Cybernetics*

Last, but certainly not least, I must mention a few obligatory words about self-esteem and self-image. One of the key ingredients in a happy, productive existence is a good self-image or high self-esteem. This is vital for both managers and employees. From the employee's perspective, it is important to avoid activities that seriously undermine one's self-esteem and self-respect. You can get away from an organization (and start over) but you can't get away from yourself. From management's perspective, it is critical to understand the importance of self-esteem and self-image to the employee. Once again, management must avoid undermining an employee's basic needs. Treat employees in a manner that will support, not undermine, their self-esteem.

Self-esteem is closely linked with self-image. To understand how people will react to certain changes or assignments, it is important to understand their self-image—how they see themselves. Management should try to make assignments, to the extent feasible, that will fit an employee's self-image. If you have an employee with a self-image of a quality perfectionist, don't assign her to a function requiring high productivity with limited quality concerns. If you have an employee with a self-image of a peace-maker, don't make him your organization's hit man.

Employees will strongly resist activities that conflict with their self-image (even where their self-image is totally distorted). Thus, it is important for management to understand how employees see themselves and manage accordingly.

While addressing self-image, let me expound upon one of the underlying objectives of this book—helping you to develop a new self-image. The first and most basic step towards being a New Age manager or employee is to start thinking of yourself as a New Age manager/employee.

The specific managerial techniques and tools you will need to use will vary from organization to organization, but the self-image is fundamental. However you may have thought of yourself in the past (whether you separated your personal identity from your work identity or allowed your work role to define your personal identity) you can create a holistic self-image that uses work as a projection of your true being. Meaning exists only within a context. Create your own context.

Start thinking of yourself as a New Age person, New Age manager, New Age employee, a social revolutionary, a peaceful warrior, a transformer, an Aquarian Conspirator, a true freedom fighter, a futurist, a spiritual evolutionist, (use whichever term appeals to you most). Once you create this new context and new self-image, the specific tools, techniques, and opportunities will come easily. But if you fail to create the new self-image and allow the traditionalists to define you as just another brick in the wall, then the techniques we have outlined in this brief book will soon be forgotten and will never be developed and put to use. This book will have failed in one of its objectives of helping you to generate meaningful change within your own work environment, and you will have wasted your time.

In summary, it is not terribly important whether you remember or use all the specific techniques outlined in this book, but it is very important that you begin to think of yourself differently and that you begin to see yourself as an Aquarian Conspirator (or whatever term you prefer) and as a force helping to create the New Age.

In Confusion

NOTE: For maximum appreciation this final section should be read while listening to a recording of "My Generation" by The Who or "Young at Heart" by Frank Sinatra depending upon your musical preferences.

The Age of Change

Today, change is occurring so fast and is so widespread that it keeps many people in a state of confusion much of the time. This brief book has been an effort to bring some clarity (by creating a context) to the radical changes taking place in the work environment (as part of the larger patterns of change in society) and to note the kinds of changes that must occur for our organizations to be effective, fun places to work.

Within the next 10 to 15 years, the first New Age generation (the Baby Boomers) and their spiritual-philosophical allies will take over virtually all of the key positions in our society. This will result in even more radical changes. This passing of the torch of leadership to a new generation is cause for alarm among many traditionalists currently in power. But the Baby Boomers and their younger and older soul-mates are eagerly awaiting this transition. Their day is coming. It cannot be stopped. The sun is rising on a New Age!

POT-SHOTS NO. 784.

SHOULD I ABIDE BY THE RULES UNTIL THEY'RE CHANGED,

OR HELP SPEED THE CHANGE BY BREAKING THEM?

© BRILLIANT ENTERPRISES 1975.

Ashleigh Brilliant

About the Author

Mr. Garland has seventeen years work experience with one of the world's largest employers. He has worked in various sections of the country from New York City to San Francisco and in a wide variety of positions including technical, public contact, supervision, personnel management, employee relations, employee development, and labor relations. He has also worked as a legislative aide in the Missouri State Senate, a district campaign coordinator for former U.S. Senator Stuart Symington, a Presidential campaign worker for Robert Kennedy, and as a student counselor.

He has a Bachelor's Degree in Education (social science major), a Master's Degree in Political Science (University of Missouri) and has done additional post-graduate work at several schools and colleges including the University of California at Berkeley.

He is the author of previous books dealing with esoteric subjects such as zen and romance and is currently working on two new books—the first explores all aspects of the New Age and is tentatively titled, "Living, Loving and Laughing in the New Age: The Continuing Saga of the Aquarian Conspiracy or How to Relax and Enjoy the Planetary Transformation" and the second deals again with work and is tentatively titled "Making Work Fun: Increasing Morale Without Increasing Costs."

His entrepreneurial projects have included a travel service, a publishing company, a meditation center, and currently a management/worker consulting firm.

He presently lives in the San Francisco Bay Area with his wife and daughter.

For information about workshops, seminars, and consultation services available from the author (on such topics as: New Age Management, Making Work Fun, Making Work Meaningful, Success WITH Integrity, Enlightened Cynicism, etc), please write to him at:

Transforming Work
6114 LaSalle Avenue, Suite 283
Oakland, California 94611

Recommended Readings

Andrew Tobias wrote a helpful little book called *The Only Investment Guide You'll Ever Need*. Unfortunately, *Working and Managing in the New Age* cannot claim to be the "only management book you'll ever need." This book provides a basic conceptual framework, but you will need to fill in a lot of particulars. Therefore, throughout the book and again here, recommended readings are listed to expand your knowledge and understanding.

To be a good worker/manager you will need to continually update your knowledge. It would be a reasonable goal to read at least one new book a week. If you don't have time to read, consider audio tapes for your car. Many of the following books are available on tape and you can listen to them while you commute. Whether you read or listen to tapes in this age of information, you will need to continuously update your information and re-evaluate your assumptions and conceptual framework.

American Spirit: Visions of a New Corporate Culture by Lawrence M. Miller. William Morrow & Company, 1984, NY

The Aquarian Conspiracy: Personal and Social Transformation in the 1980's by Marilyn Ferguson. J.P. Tarcher, Inc., 1980 **L. A.**

The Basic Ideas of Science of Mind by Ernest Holmes. Science of Mind Publications, 1957 L.A.

Chop Wood, Carry Water: A Guide to Finding Spiritual Fulfillment in Everyday Life by Rick Fields, Peggy Taylor, Rex Weyler and Rick Ingrasci. Jeremy P. Tarcher, Inc, 1984 L.A.

Creating Excellence: Managing Corporate Culture, Strategy, and Change in the New Age by Craig Hickman and Michael Silva. New American Library, 1984 NY

Creative Work: Karma Yoga by Edmond Szekely. International Biogenic Society, 1973 Costa Rica

126

Dress for Success by John T. Molloy, Warner Books, 1975, NY

The Foundations of Unity by Frank B. Whitney. Unity Church, Unity Village, Missouri

Future Shock by Alvin Toffler. Random House, 1970 NY

Getting to Yes: Negotiating Agreement Without Giving In by Roger Fisher and William Ury. Penguin Inc, 1981 NY

The Greening of America by Charles A. Reich. Random House, 1970 NY

Handbook to Higher Consciousness by Ken Keyes, Jr. Living Love Publications 1975 Coos Bay Oregon

How to Make Meetings Work: The New Interaction Method by Michael Doyle and David Straus. Berkley Publishing Group, 1976 NY

How to Make Your Life Work by Ken Keyes, Jr. Living Love Publications Coosbay, OR 1974

In Search of Excellence by Thomas Peters and Robert Waterman. Harper & Row 1982 NY

The Joy of Stress by Dr. Peter G. Hanson. Andrews, McMeel, & Parker 1985 Kansas City

The Joy of Working by Denis Waitley and Reni Witt. Ballantine Books, 1985 NY

Leader Effectiveness Training by Dr. Thomas Gordon. Wyden Books, 1977 Chicago

Leaders by Warren Bennis and Burt Nanus. Harper & Row, 1985 NY

Listening: The Forgotten Skill by Madelyn Burley-Allen. John Wiley & Sons Inc 1982 NY

Molloy's Live for Success by John T. Molloy. Bantam Books, 1981 NY

The Power of Positive Thinking by Dr. Norman Vincent Peale. Simon & Schuster 1987 New York

Re-inventing the Corporation: Transforming Your Job and Your Company for the New Information Society by John Naisbitt and Patricia Aburdene. Warner Books, 1985, New York

The Road Less Traveled by M. Scott Peck. Simon & Schuster, 1978, NY

Skillful Means by Tarthang Tulku. Dharma Publishing, 1978, Berkeley CA

Small is Beautiful: Economics as if People Mattered by E. F. Schumacher. Harper & Row, 1973, New York

Start Living Every Day of Your Life by Margaret R. Stortz. Science of Mind Publication 1981 LA

Stress without Distress by Hans Selye. New American Library, 1974, NY

The Tao of Leadership: Leadership Strategies for a New Age by John Heider. Humanics New Age 1986 GA

The Third Wave by Alvin Toffler. Bantam Books, 1980 NY

Top Performance by Zig Ziglar. Fleming H. Revell Company, 1986 New Jersey

The Turning Point: Science, Society, and the Rising Culture by Fritjof Capra. Simon & Schuster, 1982 NY

Upwingers: A Futurist Manifesto by F. M. Esfandiary. John Day Company 1973 NY

What Color is Your Parachute? A Practical Manual for Job-Hunters and Career Changers by Richard Nelson Bolles. Ten Speed Press Berkeley 1982 CA

Whole-Brain Thinking: Working from Both Sides of the Brain to Achieve Peak Job Performance by Jacquelyn Wonder and Priscilla Donovan. Ballantine Books, 1984 NY

Winning at Office Politics by Andrew Dubrin. Ballantine Books, 1978 NY

Wishcraft: How to Get What You Really Want by Barbara Sher and Annie Gottlieb. Ballantine Books, 1979 NY

The Woman's Dress for Success Book by John T. Molloy. Warner Books 1977 NY

Work and Love: The Critical Balance by Jay Rohrlich. Harmony Books, 1980 NY

Working and Liking It by Richard Germann, Diane Blumenson, and Peter Arnold. Fawcett/Columbine/Ballantine, 1984 NY

Zen and the Art of Motorcycle Maintenance by Robert Pirsig. Bantam Books, 1974 NY

Recommended Readings - by Chapter

Chapter 1

The Aquarian Conspiracy: Personal and Social Transformation in the 1980's by Marilyn Ferguson. This is the definitive analysis of the New Age. More than any other book on the subject, this one creates a context for understanding the full implications of the New Age.

Future Shock and *The Third Wave* by Alvin Toffler. Both of these works are excellent and provide many insights into the changes taking place in the world today.

Upwingers: A Futurist Manifesto by F. M. Esfandiary. In some ways, this book is an attack on certain "New Age" ideas, but it is important to consider opposing and alternate views and this one is thought-provoking.

The Greening of America by Charles A. Riech. It is now somewhat dated (written in 1970), but it still contains many valid ideas and helps to show the way our understanding of the "New Age" has progressed.

The Turning Point: Science, Society, and the Rising Culture by Fritjof Capra. This is another excellent, comprehensive analysis of the radical shift which is occurring in the way we look at the world.

American Spirit: Visions of a New Corporate Culture by Lawrence M. Miller. One of the best books ever written on management in the modern age. Miller's themes are leadership and purpose, and he argues that creating purpose is the first priority of managers in the New Age.

Chapter 3
Recommended Readings

The Tao of Leadership: Leadership Strategies for a New Age by John Heider. This is an enlightening book patterned after Lao Tzu's classic *Tao Te Ching.* Chapters 29, "The Paradox of Pushing" and 30, "Force and Conflict" are especially good.

Creating Excellence: Managing Corporate Culture, Strategy, and Change in the New Age by Craig Hickman and Michael Silva. Especially recommended is Chapter 10 "Patience: Living in the Long Term."

Leaders by Warren Bennis and Burt Nanus. Major focus is on the difference between managers and leaders and the need for more leadership and less management. Highly Recommended.

In Search of Excellence by Thomas Peters and Robert Waterman. It has become a modern classic. Well worth reading.

Leader Effective Training by Dr. Thomas Cordon. This was the first book they gave me when I first became a supervisor and I still refer to it regularly.

Top Performance by Zig Ziglar. He certainly supports the positive attitude approach and he has an especially good section on performance problems.

Small is Beautiful: Economics as if People Mattered by E. F. Schumacher. Another classic. What an idea—economics as if people mattered.

Re-inventing the Corporation: Transforming Your Job and Your Company for the New Information Society by John Naisbitt and Patricia Aburdene. Mr. Naisbitt also wrote the excellent and highly recommended book, *Megatrends. Re-inventing* is one of the best books available on changes in the work environment.

131

Chapter 4: Career Objectives
Recommended Readings

What Color Is Your Parachute? A Practical Manual for Job-Hunters and Career Changers by Richard Bolles. This book will help you find your purpose in life and identify your best skills.

Wishcraft: How to Get What You Really Want by Barbara Sher and Annie Gottlieb. This is another excellent book which will help you identify your true objectives and goals and help you devise realistic ways to achieve them.

Work as Meditation

How to Meditate by Lawrence LeShan. An excellent introduction to the many types of meditation.

Inclusive

Working and Liking It by Richard Germann, Diane Blumenson, and Peter Arnold. It is the ultimate book on job tailoring or job restructuring.

Chop Wood, Carry Water: A Guide to Finding Spiritual Fulfillment in Everyday Life by Rick Fields, Peggy Taylor, Rex Weyler and Rick Ingrasci. This is an absolute must. It not only has an excellent chapter on work but covers the full range of human activities in a delightful and informative manner.

Zen and the Art of Motorcycle Maintenance by Robert Pirsig. Contains an interesting discussion of the importance of quality in all activities.

Foundations of Unity by Frank B. Whitney. One in a series of source books from the Church of Unity, a New Thought Christian school.

Start Living Every Day of Your Life by Margaret R. Stortz. Reverend Stortz is the pastor of the Church of Religious Science in Oakland, California. She has also written several excellent pamphlets which explain in detail the Science of Mind.

Creative Work: Karma Yoga by Edmond Szekely. This is a small book with some big ideas. Karma Yoga involves union through work.

Chapter 5
Recommended Readings

The Joy of Working by Denis Waitley and Reni Witt. This is a delightful book that starts positive and becomes progressively more positive.

Skillful Means by Tarthang Tulku. This book deals with how to make work a path to enjoyable living.

The Road Less Traveled by M. Scott Peck. This book doesn't deal directly with work at all. However, it is an outstanding study of human nature and human needs.

The Power of Positive Thinking by Dr. Norman Vincent Peale. Still a classic.

The Basic Ideas of Science of Mind by Ernest Holmes. Mr. Holmes founded the Church of Religious Science which is part of the New Thought Christian movement.

How to Make Your Life Work by Ken Keyes, Jr. and Bruce Burkan. Under the first key, "Positive Attitude" we quoted an extended excerpt from Mr. Keyes outstanding guide *Handbook to Higher Consciousness* and provided information on ordering it. This book listed here is a brief summary of the ideas in the *Handbook*. This is a good introduction. Entertaining and informative. Mr. Keyes also has several other books. All are recommended.

A Whack on the Side of the Head: How to Unlock Your Mind for Innovation by Roger von Oech. Excellent book on creativity which notes the vital role that fun and humor play in the effective work environment.

Chapter 6: Meetings
Recommended Reading

How to Make Meetings Work: The New Interaction Method by Michael Doyle and David Straus
The Interaction Method was developed, in part, through work at the Western Program Service Center in Northern California. The book covers all aspects of meetings including agendas, who should attend, conduct of the meeting, structure, setting, etc.

Unions

Mutual Gains: A Guide to Union-Management Cooperation by Edward Cohen-Rosenthal and Cynthia Burton. A good comprehensive guide to management-union cooperation.

Negotiations

Getting to Yes: Negotiating Agreement Without Giving In by Roger Fisher and William Ury. This is *the* book on negotiating. It details the method of "principled negotiating" developed at the Harvard Negotiations Project. The focus is on deciding issues based on merits rather than haggling.

Clothes

Dress for Success, the Women's Dress for Success Book, and *Molloy's Live for Success* by John T. Molloy. Molloy's books are based on research, not personal opinion.

Recommended Readings

Lawyers

29 Reasons Not to go to Law School by Ralph Warner and Toni Ihara. This is a delightful book which promises to save you 3 years, $30,000, and your sanity if you are even considering law school.

Stress

The Joy of Stress by Dr. Peter G. Hanson. This is one of the best books available on all aspects of stress, how to cope and use stress to your advantage.

Stress without Distress by Hans Selye. This book deals with the need for balance between too much and too little stress.

Careerists

Work and Love: The Critical Balance by Jay Rohrlich. Contains a detailed discussion of workaholics.

Organizational Politics

Winning at Office Politics by Andrew Dubrin. Discusses various strategies for the smart office politician and explains ways for organizations to minimize political activity.

Women

The Androgynous Manager: Blending Male and Female Management Styles for Today's Organization by Alice G. Sargent. Available from the American Management Association.

Two Brains

Whole-Brain Thinking: Working from Both Sides of the Brain to Achieve Peak Job Performance by Jacquelyn Wonder and Priscilla Donavan.

Culture

Corporate Cultures: The Rites and Rituals of Corporate Life by Terrence E. Deal and Allan A. Kennedy.

the Secretary

Good Bosses Do: How to Find and Keep a Good Secretary by Betsy Lazary. Tips on developing an effective manager-secretary relationship.

Working Parents

When Mothers and Fathers Work: Creative Strategies for Balancing Career and Family by Renee Magid with Nancy Fleming.

In Confusion
Recommended Reading

Do You Believe in Magic? The Second Coming of the 60's Generation by Annie Gottlieb.

About the Artist

My office walls are covered with hundreds of "Pot-Shots" (humorous, illustrated epigrams or cartoons) by Mr. Ashleigh Brilliant. I am inspired almost daily by reading one or more of these clever cards. Mr. Brilliant's epigrams have given me more insight into work and management than any 500 page book or 16 week class on the subject.

Because my ideas on work and management have been influenced to such an extent by these delightful cards and because they have given me so many smiles and laughs over the years, I am dedicating this book to Mr. Brilliant and, with his permission, sharing a few of these wonderful "Pot-Shots" in the book.

Mr. Brilliant (his real name) was born in England, graduated from the University of London, and got his Ph.D. in history at the University of California at Berkeley. He has taught history, written several books and a play, run for political office, been ousted from the Soviet Union for delivering a lecture about free speech while standing on a bucket in Red Square, and, thanks to Hallmark Cards, is the world's highest paid author at over $400 per word.

Any of the Pot-Shots in this book as well as over 4,000 more may be ordered from Brilliant Enterprises, 117 W. Valerio St., Santa Barbara, CA 93101 for 15 cents each, plus $2 for postage and handling.

MORE OUTSTANDING BOOKS FROM HUMANICS NEW AGE:

Tao of Management
Bob Messing

An age old study for New Age managers. The Tao of Management will enable managers to see how things happen in their work environment and to understand how energies flow or become blocked. Broad issues of trust, social values, and awareness provide insights into the skills and goals which provide clarity and a sense of accomplishment to the manager.

Tao of Leadership
John Heider

Group leader, program director and teacher, John Heider (Easlen Institute, Human Potential School of Mendocino, Meniger Foundation), explores the Tao Te Ching from the viewpoints of power, potential, and persuasion. From understanding yourself and others, to enhancing creativity and handling conflict, this revealing and important work is for anyone who wants to master the art of effective leadership or who seeks understanding of the nature of things.

Attitudes Make A Difference
Dutch Boling

Boling, a nationally known personality, group leader and business consultant, shares proven techniques for more effective human relations. How to develop better listening and communication skills, creative thinking and problem solving techniques. A new and exciting approach to the power of attitude effectiveness.

These books and other Humanics New Age Publications are available from booksellers or from Humanics New Age P.O. Box 7447, Atlanta Georgia, 30309, 1-800-874-8844. Call or write for your free copy of our publications brochure.